SHOUTING IN THE TEMPLE

Shouting in the Temple

A Radical Look at Children's Ministry

Lorna Jenkins

Copyright © 2018 by Lorna Jenkins

Published by CCS Publishing
23890 Brittlebush Circle
Moreno Valley, CA 92557 USA
1-888-511-9995

All rights reserved. No part of this publication may be reproduced, stored in a retrieval system, or transmitted, in any form or by any means, electronic, mechanical, photocopying, recording, or otherwise, without the prior written permission of the publisher.
Printed in the United States of America.

Cover design: Dragan Bilic

ISBN: 978-1-935789-93-2

All Scripture quotations, unless otherwise indicated, are from the Holy Bible, New International Version, Copyright ©1973, 1978, 1984 by International Bible Society. Used by permission.

CCS Publishing is the book-publishing division of Joel Comiskey Group, a resource and coaching ministry dedicated to equipping leaders for cell-based ministry. Find us on the World Wide Web at www.joelcomiskeygroup.com

CONTENTS

INTRODUCTION	11
THE PROLOGUE. THE GREAT KING'S PARTY	15
CHAPTER 1. GOD HAS A DREAM	17
How God Sees Children	20
Jesus is on Their Side	21
Children Model the Kingdom Relationship	22
God chooses Children	23
How the Church Sees Children	24
To Think About	25
CHAPTER 2. GOD'S PLAN FOR CHILDREN: THE FAMILY STRAND	27
God Places Children in Families	28
Children in the Old Testament Community	29
Why God Chose the Family.	31
The Community of Faith	31
Children in the Nation	33
Community in our Urban Society	34
The Generational Blessing	34
Family History	36
Children in the New Testament Church	39
Being Family In the Church Today	40
Why God Insists on Trusting Families	42
To Think About	43
CHAPTER 3. GOD'S PLAN FOR CHILDREN. THE STRAND OF SPIRITUAL MATURITY	45
Jesus Included Children	45
God Calls Children	47
Children Are Empowered	49

| What God is Doing with Children in This Generation | 51 |
| To Think About | 55 |

INTERLUDE. THE PARABLE OF THE ENEMY CONQUEROR 57

CHAPTER 4. THE SPIRITUAL BATTLE FOR CHILDREN 59
The Mutilation of the Family	61
The Breaking of Generational Lines	62
The Rise of Secularism	64
Children's Feelings About Church	66
To Think About	67

FLASHBACK. THE CHURCH IN THE HOUSE OF MARCELLUS 69

CHAPTER 5. (FOR THOSE WHO LIKE HISTORY) WHAT HAPPENED IN THE PAST 73
The Church Became an Institution	74
The Reformation and Children	75
The Children of Revival	76
The Rise of the Sunday School	79
To Think About	81

CHAPTER 6. A CHILD'S EYE VIEW OF CHURCH 83
What Children See in Church 84
   1. The Divided Families 84
   2. The Shallow Relationships 86
   3. Separation From the Adults 87
   4. There is No Sense of Awe in the Church 87
   5. Knowing is More Important than Living 88
   6. How Children See the Pastor 90
   7. The Silence in the Homes 90
   8. Children From Outside the Church 91
To Think About 92

CHAPTER 7. A CHURCH WHERE CHILDREN BELONG 93
   1. Family Life 95
   2. Cell Group Life 95
   3. Celebration 95
   4. Equipping Track 95
An Old Testament Example 96

To Think About 97

CHAPTER 8. INTERGENERATIONAL CHURCH. VISIONING, PLANNING, CREATING, TRAINING 99
The Beginning of the Journey 100
Strategies To Achieve The Vision 101
Strategies for Children's Ministry in Faith Community Baptist Church. 102
The Process of Change 103
God Moved Us To Intergenerational Cells 104
Stages of the Transition. 105
The Senior Pastor's Role 105
   (a) Proclamation 105
   (b) The Guardian of the Vision 106
The Pilot Group 107
Training Meetings 109
   (a) Parents 109
   (b) Children's leaders – Sunday School teachers. 110
Church Changes flowing from Intergenerational Groups 111
Positive Effects of Intergenerational Cells. 113
What about the Youth? 114
The Whole Picture 116
To Think About 116

INTERLUDE. THE INTERGENERATIONAL EXPERIENCE 119

CHAPTER 9. LEARNING TO OPERATE INTERGENERATIONAL CELLS 125
Practising Intergenerational Cells with Children 126
Obstacles That Often Arise 129
   (a) Behavior 129
   (b) Age Differences 131
   (c) Including the Younger Children. 133
   (d) Leadership of the Kids' Slot 134
   (e) Space and Time 135
   (f) Multiplication of Intergenerational Cells 137
   (g) Some Blessings We Didn't Expect 138
Is It Worth The Effort Of The Change? 139
To Think About 140

CHAPTER 10. CHILDREN'S CELL GROUPS 141
A Stepping Stone to Intergenerational Cells 141
Class or Cell-group? 143

Looking to the Future 144
To Think About 145

CHAPTER 11. WORSHIP AND CELEBRATION 147
The Problem with Children in the Church 148
Nursery/Pre-School 150
Junior Primary Celebration 151
The Bible Message 153
The Intermediates – The Barnabas Club 155
Celebration with the Adults 156
    1. Worship and Prayer 157
    2. The Bible Message 158
    3. Memory Verse 160
    4. Helping Children to Worship in the Cell Group 161
To Think About 162

CHAPTER 12. GETTING TO KNOW CHILDREN AND MAKING THEM YOUR FRIENDS 163
Steps in Making Friends with a Child 164
    1. Conversation Openers 164
    2. Finding Common Ground 164
    3. Sharing Life Stories 165
    4. Share Your Hopes and Dreams 166
    5. Warning! 167
    6. Sharing the Lives of Children. 168
    7. Keeping the Attention of the Group 168
    8. The Floor is a Great Leveller 169
    9. The Power of Praise 170
    10. The Power of Prayer 171
    11. Encouraging Children to Talk 172
    12. The Hidden Message 173
To Think About 176

PART THREE. THE SPIRITUAL GROWTH OF CHILDREN 177
A Child's Faith – A personal testimony 177

CHAPTER 13. SPIRITUAL AWARENESS STARTS IN THE FAMILY 179
Thinking Our Way Back To Childhood 180
Finding God in the Imagination 181
    1. Someone is in Charge 181
    2. The World Ought To Be Fair 182

3. God, the Super-parent 183
4. What is Right and Wrong? 185
5. What Do Children Understand by Salvation? 187
6. Forgiveness and Restoring Peace 188
7. Positive and Negative Words 189
Adopting the Family World View 190
To Think About 191

CHAPTER 14. STAGES OF BELIEF AND DISBELIEF 193
Stages of Faith 193
  1. Received Faith 193
  2. Factual Faith 194
  3. Future Faith 197
Stages of Disbelief 199
  1. One World-view 199
  2. Challenged Faith 199
  3. Two Compartment World 201
  4. Breaking Point 203
To Think About 204

CHAPTER 15. HOW CHILDREN RECEIVE SALVATION 205
Bringing a Child to the Point of Decision 207
The Steps of a Faith Decision. 207
Muddled Pictures of Salvation 209
Do The Decisions of the Very Young Mean Anything? 211
Anxious Parents 212
To Think About 213

CHAPTER 16. NURTURING AND MENTORING 215
The Advantages of a Christian Home 215
The Downside of a Christian Background 216
No Repentance, No Gratitude 219
What is the World Like? 220
How Much Do Our Children Need to Know? 223
Children from Non-Church Homes 223
Too Many Children 225
To Think About 227

CHAPTER 17. AN EQUIPPING TRACK FOR CHILDREN 229
The Equipping Track Framework. 230
  Stage 1: 1. Point of Decision 231
  Stage 1: 2. The Journey Guide 232

Stage 1: 3. Basic Discipling	233
Stage 1: 4. Daily Time With God	234
Stage 2 of the Equipping Track:	234
1. Cell Group Participation	234
2. Christian Family Values	235
3. Understanding and Sharing the Lord's Supper	237
Stage 2: Sharing the Gospel	238
Stage 3 of the Equipping Track. 1. Spiritual Formation	240
Stage 3: 2. Sermon Notes	241
Stage 3: 3. Spiritual Warfare	242
Stage 3: 4. Bible Overview	243
CONCLUSION	245
To Think About	245

INTRODUCTION

This book explains the vision for children, which God has given me. After I had been serving in Sunday Schools for 25 years, I began to feel a deep uneasiness about the way we were doing children's ministry. I met others with questions similar to mine. The loss of children from our churches was alarming. Churches wanted answers; none of those we tested seemed to work.

For a while I co-operated with my friend, Rev. Trevor Ross in trying a few experiments in the Holland Park Baptist Church in Brisbane, Australia. When he set up children's small groups, we found there was a rapid rise in the enthusiasm and participation of the children. Dr Ralph Neighbour was also encouraging cell churches in our part of the world. His enthusiasm set me on a quest to find out how children fit into a cell church. Dr Robert Banks invited me to see the work among children of his house churches near Canberra.

At the end of our ministry in Australia, there was an unexpected opportunity for my husband and me to study at Columbia International University in South Carolina. We were among the first doctoral students in the college. I was assigned to the supervision of Dr Ron Habermas whose understanding and support I shall always appreciate. He set me free to pursue the answers to my questions. Is a cell model for children Biblical?

Is it educationally valid? Has it ever happened before? Is it happening anywhere in the world now? As I put together my dissertation, I felt a rising excitement that my vision was not only viable, but had roots in the Bible, in history and in education.

In 1993 I joined the staff of Faith Community Church in Singapore, a church that was seriously applying the cell church model. This has been a serendipity experience for me. We dreamed, worked and learned together to refine the vision into a working model. Faith Community Baptist Church was my laboratory. I was able to test my theories. I was allowed to make mistakes and try again. The staff became my allies in putting this vision into practice, especially the Children's Ministry staff. Rev Lawrence Khong led his amazing church into a style of Children's Ministry that has revolutionized my ideas of where children belong in the church.

This radical vision is not mine alone. Many people have prayed for me and challenged me to think further and higher. The children keep stretching my expectations beyond my imagination. Most of all I appreciate my husband, Brian, who has put up with long absences, and many extra chores while I have pursued my vision. He has always believed in me.

I would not have embarked on this journey, if I had not had the clear call of God. I was on the wrong side of 50 when I started. When I grew tired, God inspired me with new energy and hope. Now I look forward to a new generation of leaders who will continue to follow the radical vision for the children of the Kingdom.

Lorna Jenkins, 1999

Fifteen years later I am looking back on the children of our ministry, who are emerging into adulthood. On a recent trip to Singapore I was delighted to see many of the children I knew, are now leading the church in worship, and in the ministry team of the church. Some of the original children's staff are still in leadership. Some are "retiring" to share their experience with other churches and organizations in the city. Their replacements are people who have grown through the ministry. The dropout rate has been minimal. The passion for winning and keeping children is still strong.

The church has moved to a different model of cell church. Inevitably this has affected the intergenerational cells. The church still takes seriously the equipping of the children to become fully operational members of the body of Christ.

There is no doubt that intergenerational cell groups are a labour-intensive, demanding form of cell group. However, their impact on the lives of the children is enormous. Some churches have tried to modify the intergenerational content of their ministry to the children but it is not easy to maintain if there is no planned event where the children and adults can meet.

The encouraging trend I am seeing today, is that a vast number of churches are now striving to lead the children into the day-by-day practice of the Christian faith, rather than just instructing them. Children are being trained to pray effectively, to worship, to share their faith with their friends, to read the Bible for themselves, and to trust God in their problems of life. If they discover that God is alive and able to meet their need while they are still children, they will continue to know his reality and power in their teen and young adult years.

At last many churches are keen to make the children a recognized and welcome part of the congregation. We are going to need their leadership and power in the coming days.

Lorna Jenkins, 2017

THE PROLOGUE
THE GREAT KING'S PARTY

The great King decided to give a party, a splendid party that would include everyone in his Kingdom. His messengers travelled far and wide, distributing invitations so that no one would be forgotten. The invitations clearly stated that on the day of the party, the King would be giving a gift to every person in the land.

People were bubbling with excitement. Everyone planned to be there, for no one wanted to miss the King's gift. What would it be? A piece of land? A gold coin? A precious stone?

The parents worried about their children. They did not want to miss the King's party, yet they were reluctant to bring them. Suppose they misbehaved and made their parents feel ashamed? If the children were present, Mom and Dad would spend their time cutting up food, cleaning up spills and settling arguments. It would be far better if the children were not there. Therefom they decided to give the children a party of their own at the same time as the King's party.

On the day of the great event, everyone wore their finest clothes. The children were delivered to the children's party, while the adults waited for the King to arrive. Entering quietly, he saw that everyone was enjoying the feast, but there were no children present.

"Where are the children?" he asked one of the servants.

"Oh Sire, the parents have made a special party for the children by themselves. They are in the hall across the street having a good time.

The King frowned and left as quietly as he had entered. He crossed the street to where the children were.

They were so excited to see him! They asked him to play with them and he took time to talk with each one of them and give each child a gift. "Now," he said, "let's go back to my other party."

By this time the adults were wondering where the king was. "How strange that he invited us to a party, and yet he is not here."

At that moment the doors opened and the King arrived, followed by a host of children. They were singing and smiling and waving their gifts.

"We cannot understand it," thought the parents. "Why would the King rather be with the children than with us?"

Then they began to wonder what the King had given to their children — perhaps some candy or toys?

The King walked to the front and spoke to them. "My people. When I invited all my people to my party, I meant everyone, no matter how old or young. I have gifts for each of you, especially for those young enough to receive them.

When the parents looked at their children's gifts they were astonished. Some had received a gift of Wisdom; others a gift of Prophecy. Some had been given a gift of Healing, some, a gift of Prayer. Others had Encouragement; still others, Helping. The children were delighted. They thought it only natural that the King would give them such gifts to use.

The parents were amazed. The children's gifts were exactly like theirs.

Chapter 1

GOD HAS A DREAM

Through ageless centuries, God has had a dream. In His mind his Kingdom has already come. His reign is established. Those who love him rejoice in his presence and serve him. Young and old, men and women, they encompass every race and rank. Among them is a host of joyous children, serving him energetically and obeying him with their whole hearts.

In our world we cannot see God's dream. We are too hedged in by the pressures of the society we know. Yet every time we pray, "Thy Kingdom come", we are affirming His dream. When will it become real on earth as it is in heaven?

Our churches have become accustomed to children who are cheerful, noisy and mostly bored with God. We hope they will be different when they grow up but we don't expect much of them now. Our expectations for them are insignificant, compared with the dreams God has for them. If they really knew God, they wouldn't be bored with him.

I grew up in a small community of Reading Brethren who had not heard about Christian Education. They made no concessions to my limited understanding. I sang their hymns and learned their vocabulary. I sat through long sessions of "preaching to the saints". I would count the bricks on the wall and make puzzles out of the numbers in the hymnbooks.

Yet unconsciously these people fulfilled one aspect of God's dream. They were my spiritual family. Each of them loved me and I knew it. They knew my name, my school class, my pets and my friends. Brother Boulton was a gruff old man who preached well past the appointed hour, but he also took me on his knee so I could hear his watch tick. I helped his wife make biscuits.

There was old Miss Beauchamp, who wore a velvet ribbon round her throat. She always had a bag of sweets for children who had behaved well in the "Morning Meeting." Frequently families invited us to Sunday dinner, or sometimes they would come to our home. I still have a book given to me by a "sister" who wanted to comfort me when I was recovering from whooping cough.

Years later, when I had tried all kinds of ways to make church more interesting for a new generation of children, I found myself wondering why they got less pleasure out of church than I did. I used to stand on the seats and sing the hymns loudly, sliding over the words I couldn't understand. I held my mother's coat during the Lord's Supper, just in case He might come again and forget to take me too.

Today's children do not sing or pray in church. Often they do not even stand. It is only too obvious that coming to church was not their idea. Their most fervent prayer is for it to be over quickly.

Churches release their children to Children's Church quickly so that they will not disturb the adult's worship. Parents are relieved to see them go. A dynamic program is arranged to keep them happy while the service continues. The intention is that they will learn some Bible stories, play some games and enjoy themselves enough so that some day they will be willing enough to belong to the church.

However, many children around the world are leaving the church at the first opportunity. Some years ago we did a survey in New Zealand across all the denominations, to see what happens to our children. It revealed that of the children who are born into Christian homes, 80 per cent never become active adult members. In Australia one denomination estimated that 94 per cent of its children leave the church before they are adults. There is no reason to believe that the figures would be any better today in most of the Western world. We still hear sad parents whose hearts are aching for their unbelieving children.

In the years since we did that survey I have had the opportunity to visit many other countries of the world. The church is no longer an exclusively Western phenomenon. People from all the continents have discovered the power of God to transform lives. They would not recognize the picture of children in the churches, which I have described above. In many places it never occurred to the people to isolate the children from the main body of God's people. The children learned from what they saw the grown-ups doing. In different countries and cultures, we are beginning to see God's vision coming true. The church is looking young again.

In my twenty-five years of trying to make Sunday School work, I trained diligently. I learned to communicate with creative arts, puppets, and dance. I honed my story-telling skills. I sat on committees and wrote lesson material. I trained others to copy what I did. But for all the effort and creativity and dedication of the leaders, Sunday school was not working.

That's what drove me back to the Bible to rediscover God's dream. He did not plan to bring them into the world so that they might eventually be lost. They belong to him.

HOW GOD SEES CHILDREN

When a child decides to follow Jesus, God jumps for joy! He or she will have time to discover what God is like, before the world has a chance is distract them.

God has an overwhelming belief in the importance of children. That's why he assigns a heavenly being to watch over a child from the moment of his or her conception.[1]

If anyone turns a child away, God gets angry. He would sooner a person die on the spot than spoil another young life.[2] Yet every day children are being turned away for trivial reasons, before they know Who they are rejecting. We understand how God feels. We also get angry if anyone ignores or harms a child.

Mostly we do it unconsciously. We are so keen on our own agendas, we desire so much to inspire the adult congregation, that we tend to see the children as a disturbance and distraction. Even parents long for a few minutes of peace in church, without their children.

---

1. Matthew 18:10
2. Matthew 18:6

JESUS IS ON THEIR SIDE

Jesus warned us to be careful about the way we treat children. The way we treat them is the way we treat him! "When you welcome little ones like these," he said, "you are welcoming me."[3]

He has chosen to be on their side. He identifies with them as he always does with those who are dependant and have no voice. Perhaps he finds himself most comfortable in the back hall where they are playing.

When children enter our churches we want to change them. By our attitudes we say, "All we ask of you while you are here is that you keep quiet. You don't have to listen, or pay attention, or participate, One day you can be one of us, when you can understand what the preacher says and when you can behave exactly like us."

However, Jesus said "Unless we change and become like little children, we cannot enter the Kingdom of Heaven."[4] This statement seems strange to many adults. Does it mean we should play with toys and be childish? Should we behave like children and fight with each other and throw tantrums?

Jesus was not talking about behaviour but about status. The disciples had been arguing about who would be greatest in Heaven. Jesus stood a child in the midst of them as an illustration about the Kingdom.

I believe this was symbolic. Children belong in the midst of the family of God, not around the edges. They should

---

3. Matthew 18:5
4. Matthew 18:3

be living under the protection of their parents and their spiritual community. They should be visible to the church, partly so that we cannot overlook them, but also because they constantly remind us of what the Kingdom is like. Otherwise we tend to forget the model and to remould the Kingdom into a kingdom of this world.

CHILDREN MODEL THE KINGDOM RELATIONSHIP

By a miracle, which we call 'new birth', we enter into a new relationship with God – one with family ties. We may grow older or wiser, more educated or even more spiritual, but our relationship with God remains the same. We are children and he is Father. Once we are prepared to acknowledge our status in the Kingdom as children, then we are the greatest – along with all the others. That is the only status there is.

We need to treat God as Father. Little children trust a good father. He cares for them and provides their needs, and they give him their love and obedience. God asks only two things of children. They should honour their parents and obey them. In the Kingdom we all have the same two responsibilities: to honour our Father God and to obey him.

There are no second-class citizens in the Kingdom. Children do not become citizens when they grow up. They are citizens now, with rights and responsibilities. As parents and members of their spiritual family, our task is to help them learn the Kingdom life-style while they are children.

After all, the Kingdom of Heaven is theirs.[5] They have not earned it or worked for it; they have inherited it as their birthright. This is what God planned. It's not just that he

---
5. Luke 18:16

values them as leaders of the future. He likes them and wants them to be in his kingdom now. He loves hearing their praise, just as we love to hear our children say, "I love you, Daddy." He calls them to serve him and he trusts them with ministry that we normally reserve for adults.

Many people think they ought to entertain children when they come to church, otherwise they might not want to come. God has a better plan. He wants them to be fully part of the family, sharing the fun and helping with the responsibilities. For him their lives have endless possibilities for good.

GOD CHOOSES CHILDREN

When God is planning a significant move in this world he often starts by choosing a child. He prepares and trains the child for his mission and purpose. He also makes promises through children.

Abraham's son, Isaac, was a child of promise; he became the founder of a great nation.[6] Moses was rescued as a baby to become Israel's deliverer from the Egyptians.[7] Samson was chosen before his birth to be a deliverer.[8]

Samuel was set aside as a child for a prophetic and priestly role.[9] David was little more than a lad, when he was anointed to be king.[10] John the Baptist was chosen while still a child to prepare the way for the coming Messiah.[11]

---

6. Genesis 18:17-19
7. Hebrews 11:23
8. Judges 13:5
9. I Samuel 1:11
10. I Samuel 16:11
11. Luke 1:76

God did not despise childhood, but chose to enter the world through the body of a baby.[12] He might have arrived as an adult prophet, appearing out of the desert of Judea but he chose the longer, harder way.

Jesus had to grow up in a human family, just like most of us. God had to accept the limitations of childhood. He had to learn to walk and talk, to live among human brothers and sisters, to read and write in Hebrew, to work and take responsibility in his family. He had to learn to obey his parents. He understands what it is like to be three, or eight, or eleven.

HOW THE CHURCH SEES CHILDREN

The church no longer sees children as signs of promise. We tend to see them as problems to the ministry. At best they are a recruiting pool for the future. A thriving Sunday School foreshadows a thriving church.

The outcomes of children's ministry are seldom reviewed. Did the children from Christian homes, grow up to follow Jesus and become part of his church, or have they disappeared without trace? What about the children from outside the church family, who also believed in Jesus?

When children stay, it is because they are wanted. It is not because they enjoyed the program, but because the people loved them and treated them as part of the family.
One long-established inner-city church was childless. It had declined to under 50 members, all over sixty years of age. At one member's meeting an elderly gentleman said, "Friends, if

---

12. Isaiah 9:6

God does not give us some children, this church won't be here twenty years from now. Let's ask the Lord for some children." They began to pray earnestly that God would send them children. "Lord," they said, "we don't care if they're noisy, if they run around. We promise we'll love them and make them feel at home. We don't even care if we need to change our worship service. Please give us some children."

A couple of months later a family visited. The children discovered they had a family of spiritual grandparents so they wanted to stay. Another family heard about the church, so they came to try it out. One by one other children began to come and the church found new life.

A church without children is doomed to die. Clearly God thinks children are important and he has specific plans for how they should be nurtured. We need to re-discover his plans.

TO THINK ABOUT

1. How do the adults in your church regard the children? Are they,
(a) Disturbers of the peace?
(b) A constant drain on leaders and helpers?
(c) The source of a vital youth work?
(d) The victims of marriage conflict or parental abuse?
(e) Part of God's family who can love him and serve him now?

2. Write down the names of as many children as you know in your church.
What is the total? Do you know anything about them? Do they greet you as a friend?

3. Can you think of any child in your church who might be "a child of promise". Have you ever prayed for the spiritual destiny of the children in your church or family?

Chapter 2

GOD'S PLAN FOR CHILDREN: THE FAMILY STRAND

Young Joel was working with his Dad in the potter's shed. It was still only afternoon, but already Dad was packing up his tools and cleaning his potter's wheel. "Why are we finishing so early?" asked Joel.

"We must get ready for Passover," Dad answered. "Your mother's been preparing for it all day. Haven't you seen her washing the clothes and the dishes and the whole house? At sundown we'll begin to remember the Passover feast. There's a lot to do."

"I saw you kill the lamb this morning. Father. I felt like crying. I can remember when it was born."

"The lamb was a special lamb, Joel. It was perfect, the best in the flock. When it died it was dying instead of us. Our sins can't be forgiven unless a perfect lamb dies. Your mother is cooking it for the Passover meal tonight. Do you remember your part? It's very important?"

"I remember I have to say, "Father, what do these things mean?"

"That's right, son. Don't forget when the time comes and then I'll tell you the story about how God rescued our ancestors from their slavery in Egypt."

"Why do you always tell the same story, Father? There are other good stories about our ancestors that I'd like to hear."

Yes, but this story tells us how God rescued his people and brought us into our own land. We must never forget how powerful and kind our God is. I can remember my father telling us the story, and now I tell it to you. One day you'll tell it to your children. That's how the story gets passed on. I'll tell you other stories another day. Now it's time for us to go inside, wash ourselves and put on our clean clothes."

GOD PLACES CHILDREN IN FAMILIES

God's plan for children has two strands. The first is based on family.

God did not design the family just as a channel of food and protection. It is a small intergenerational community in which the children learn the basic skills of living with others. They learn values and traditions and the morals acceptable in their society. They also learn of the origins of their people and their belief about God. Parents are called to be story-tellers, passing on the message of who God is and what he has done for us.

Moses said:

> "Hear, O Israel: The Lord our God, the Lord is one. Love the Lord your God with all your heart and with all your soul and with all your strength. These commandments that I give you today are

to be upon your hearts. Impress them on your children. Talk about them when they sit at home and when you walk along the road, when you lie down and when you get up. Tie them as symbols on your hands and bind them on your foreheads. Write them on the door frames of your houses and on your gates." (Deut. 6:4-9)

We should notice when God said this. He was proclaiming the first and greatest commandment to the people of Israel. He was calling for their total commitment, giving the word that would unify Jewish people through the centuries.

His very next word was for the children. His commandment was for them too. It was not to die out, but was to be handed down from generation to generation, within families and last forever.

He told parents how they should teach their children – in the normal routine of family life, when they got up in the morning, when they went to bed at night, when they came out and when they went in. The story of God's love was to be passed on in the midst of life, not in a classroom. Their family were the teachers and the children could witness how they were living out God's commandments every day.

CHILDREN IN THE OLD TESTAMENT COMMUNITY

In the average Hebrew home, this is how it worked out. Joel, the potter's son would wake up to daily prayer. He would wash himself, dress and eat food prepared according to God's commandments.

Every week the family remembered the Lord together. On Fridays they prepared for the Sabbath – cleaning the house and cooking, washing their clothes and themselves. No work was done on the Sabbath so they could remember the Lord.

Joel shared in all the big family events; the birth of a child, a marriage, a funeral. If someone committed a sin, the whole family would go to the temple or shrine, to make a sacrifice to atone for the sin. Breaking God's law was a serious matter and the children knew it.

Learning about God was part of their daily lives. It was both planned and unplanned. Teachable moments could arise at any time, especially since memorials of God's mighty acts were scattered all around them. Sometimes as they walked along the road, they might ask about a pile of stones. "Why is that pile of stone there?"

"That reminds us of how our ancestors crossed the river Jordan without getting their feet wet, when they entered the Promised Land." [13] Some people even wore the commandments of God, written on paper and tied to their foreheads or wrists. This was to show that God was in control of everything they thought and everything they did.

Our lives are not like that. We can go from day to day, year to year, without ever being reminded of the goodness of God, and the things He has done for our family and our nation.

In ancient Israel, God would not allow his followers to keep their lives private. His commandments were to be on their door-frames and gates. Each famiy's faith was to be apparent

---

13. Joshua 4:6

to the whole neighbourhood and not hidden behind the four walls of their houses.

In similar manner, Dr Ralph Neighbour, when he was pastoring West Memorial Baptist Church, in Houston, Texas, asked his members to put a small logo of the church on their mail boxes. Everyone in the community knew where to find the member of the church.

WHY GOD CHOSE THE FAMILY.

God's strategy in trusting the family to teach children about him, is based on sound educational foundations. To learn a lifestyle, you must be immersed in the lifestyle.

Learning about God is not a body of information, but a Kingdom lifestyle. The children needed to learn the facts about God in an environment where they could see His lifestyle being lived out around them. They know the teaching of their parents is true because they see it validated every day. If the teaching, which the children receive in church, is not being practised in the home, the children know that it is not true or it is not important. The consistency of life and word is crucial.

Teaching in the church can only happen for a short time on Sunday. Teaching in the home is both formal and informal, intentional and accidental. They learn both from the things we say, and from the things we try to cover up.

THE COMMUNITY OF FAITH

Families were not left to teach and bring up their children in isolation. It was a matter for concern for the whole community.

The people of the village would help each other bring in the harvests. Afterwards they would join to celebrate the Feast of Tabernacles.[14] thanking God for providing food for them for another year.

Joel would have enjoyed this. Every family in his village would make themselves a rough shelter from leafy branches. Then for a whole week they would sleep outside under their shelters, having fun together.

Sometimes the whole village would go up to Jerusalem to celebrate the great feasts. This was the best of all. They would take several days for the journey, camping out at night. As the people came near their destination, they would begin singing the songs of David and all the hills would echo their praise.

This happened to Jesus one day. His family and his village travelled to Jerusalem. When they returned, Jesus did not go back with them. I have often wondered how Mary and Joseph could have travelled for a whole day without realising that Jesus was not with them.[15]

I understood better when I talked with my New Zealand Maori friends.[16] Their children are seen as belonging to the tribe. They wander among the families freely. If children are at your place at mealtime, you feed them. If they fall asleep you put them to bed and later their parents will collect them.

It was probably like this with Jesus. Mary and Joseph believed he was safe within the community and did not worry. It was not till they looked through the whole community, that they

---

14. Leviticus 23:40-43
15. Luke 2: 43-46
16. Maoris are the early Polynesian people of New Zealand.

realised he was lost. In many of our churches people feel no responsibility for other people's children. They don't feel that they need to help the parents. Yet God sees children as part of the whole church.

CHILDREN IN THE NATION

Around the community was the nation. When the nation was gathered before God, the children were not excluded. When King Jehoshaphat was surrounded by his enemies, he knew his army was not strong enough to defeat them, so he called the whole nation to prayer.

> "The people of Judah came together to seek help from the Lord, indeed, they came from every town in Judah to seek Him. …All the men of Judah with their wives and children and little ones stood there before the Lord." (2 Chronicles 20:4, 13)

When the prophet Joel, was calling, the people to repentance, he told them to "bring together the elders, gather the children, those nursing at the breast" (Joel 2: 6) When Ezra read the word of God, the whole nation came to hear – men, women and children.[17]

God never overlooked the children. They were valued and included at all times. Other nations had other systems. For instance, in Sparta, children were removed from their parents and placed in military school. In Israel, the family was the environment of learning.

---

17. Ezra 10:1

COMMUNITY IN OUR URBAN SOCIETY

Are these ideals applicable only to small rural communities? Have the complexities of urban life made such methods of child nurture virtually impossible?

I believe the patterns can still be very much the same. City dwellers tend to form small urban communities based on proximity, race or shared interest. People do not visit each other's homes as much as they once did, but they still gather round social events; little league, school outings, neighbourhood barbecues.

In large congregations, members look for community in small groups of believers – the cell group. If there are no official cell groups, people still cluster in groups of congenial friends.

Children hear the words of the Lord first from their families. The teaching and example is supported by other adults and friends in the cell group. Children need to have other Christian friends, who support and encourage the family. Around them is the community of the church, a place where children are recognized and included, where they may express their faith and learn to serve alongside the adults.

Many children today do not think the adult church is in any way relevant to them or interested in them. It is something their parents do.

THE GENERATIONAL BLESSING

Not only does God see children as part of the wider family, He also sees them as part of the vertical family. We are part of a generational chain which reaches back into the history of the nation.

Tracing our ancestors has become a popular past-time, because it helps us find out who we are and where we have come from. When I was a child I read that God will punish sin to the third and fourth generation.[18] I thought that was unfair. I did not know that when people sin it often takes several generations to work itself out.

However, God also makes a wonderful promise.

> "Know therefore that the Lord, your God is God; He is the faithful God, keeping his covenant of love to a thousand generations of those who love Him and keep His commandments." (Deut 7 : 9)

Over and over He reminds us that His word is to be handed down. He is not a one generation God, but the God of Abraham, of Isaac, of Jacob. When he called Abraham to be a blessing to all nations. What did he expect him to do?

> "Abraham will surely become a great and powerful nation, and all the nations of the earth will be blessed through him. For I have chosen him so that he will direct his children and his household after him to keep the way of the Lord by doing what is right and just, so that the Lord will bring about for Abraham what He has promised him." (Gen 18: 18-19)

Abraham's power lay in what happened in his family and his descendents. That was God's strategy and it still is. Even

---

18. Deuteronomy 5:9

people who are unmarried or who have no biological children can have spiritual descendants, through their care and nurture of the young. Every person who decides to follow Jesus is a spiritual Abraham. He or she is beginning a new line of faith that can influence the world into the next century.

FAMILY HISTORY

About 140 years ago in Denmark, there was a blacksmith named Lars. He had a bad reputation as the town drunkard. Everyone knew about his swearing and his violence. One night he stumbled, half-drunk, into a hall where a meeting was being held. Somehow through the mists of alcohol, he heard the call of Jesus. He became a Christian and his life was transformed.

He needed to tell everyone of the great things that God had done for him. He told his wife and children, and they came to know Jesus. His apprentice, Hans also received Christ through his witness. Lars began to go around other villages giving his testimony. Many people saw the change in him and believed.

In time Hans, the apprentice, fell in love with the blacksmith's daughter, Martha. They married and had children but because times were hard in Denmark, they emigrated to New Zealand. They worked hard in their new country and raised a family of seven with one extra foster child, who had been orphaned in an accident.

All their children learned to follow Jesus. The youngest was my mother. She had only one child – me. I learned about Jesus from my parents from when I was a baby. I have three children. They have also heard about Jesus and learned to love him. Now they are bringing up children of their own.

Chapter 2. God's Plan for Children. The Family Strand

This story is not to focus attention on my family, but to establish a principle. One man's conversion 140 years ago is still making ripples in the world today. At a centennial family reunion there were seventy descendants of Hans and Martha and only two of them were not Christians. There is a generational blessing. That is the way God intended that it should be.

It is not confined to direct blood-lines. Grand-parents have won their grandchildren. Aunts and uncles have won their nieces and nephews. Friends and godparents have told the story to the next generation.

In the music of Psalm 78 we hear the hopes of the people of God.

> "We will not hide (these things) from their children; we will tell the next generation the praiseworthy deeds of the Lord, His power and the wonders He had done. He decreed statutes for Jacob and established the law in Israel, which He commanded our forefathers to teach their children, so that the next generation would know them, even the children yet to be born, and they in turn would tell their children. Then they would put their trust in God and would not forget his deeds but would keep his commandments." (Psalm 78: 4-7)

Every generation tells the next generation the things they have learned. This is not merely a desirable option for us who are growing old. It is a burning necessity. The Psalmist in Psalm 71:18 says,

> "Even when I am old and grey, do not forsake me, O God, till I declare Your power to the next generation, Your might to all who are to come."

He is saying, "Lord, don't let me die till I have told the children about your power and might." We seem to have lost some of that passion. I hear parents say, "I'll let my children decide what they believe when they grow older because I do not want to influence them." If we do not tell them our story, how will the ever know about our mighty God in the midst of the conflicting voices around them?

Not only do children receive their faith from the testimony of the previous generations, they also receive a generational blessing and anointing.

God's promise was extended to the descendants of Abraham.[19] Eli received a promise for his descendants, but it was withdrawn when they proved themselves utterly unworthy.[20] When King David became king, God promised that his descendants would rule forever.[21]

When God chooses to bless a person, the blessing continues to his/her descendants. Even today we see children who follow their parents' footsteps and receive the same blessing and anointing. Bramwell and Evangeline Booth inherited the same passion for lost people that their father had.

The blessing is not automatic though. It can be withdrawn as it was from the sons of Eli, if the children reject the generational anointing.

---

19. Genesis 17:7
20. I Samuel 2;30
21. II Samuel 7:12-13

CHILDREN IN THE NEW TESTAMENT CHURCH

When the church began, it carried forward the Old Testament pattern of children being part of the community. It never occurred to the disciples to set up a special ministry for them. They assumed that children would become Christians through the teaching of their parents.

In those days, childhood was not thought of as a separate stage of life. Children were people. They shared in the life of the family. Often they worked beside their parents to produce the family income. Only the very rich could afford servants to care for their children.

When a person became a Christian, it was natural for him to say, "Come to my house and tell this Good News to the whole family."[22] If a father became a Christian, the whole household did the same and they were baptized together.

The church was held in homes, so the children saw with their own eyes the things that God was doing. They saw how the Christians loved one another and shared their goods. They witnessed the coming of the Holy Spirit; they joined the church in praying for Peter to get out of prison; they watched miracles of healing. Those in Joppa saw what happened when their dear friend Dorcas died. They all knew Dorcas. She had made them many of the clothes they were wearing. While they were grieving, Peter arrived and raised her from the dead.[23] What child would ever forget that! They did not need to be told about the power of God. They saw it for themselves.

---

22. Acts 16:15, 33-34
23. Acts 10:36-42

They also saw how the believers suffered. They knew when the disciples were beaten for their faith; they heard how James was arrested and killed. Soldiers might burst in at any time and arrest their parents. When that happened other church members would take the children home and care for them. That's why James told the church to care for the widows and the orphans.[24] The children knew that to be a Christian was to risk your life.

The leaders of the church were family people. One of the requirements for leaders was to be a faithful spouse and a good parent.[25] This was more important than a theological training or even specific spiritual gifts.

The family was seen as the model of the church.[26] They were brothers and sisters under God. The same qualities, which are needed for good parenting were needed in the leadership of the church.

BEING FAMILY IN THE CHURCH TODAY

It is hard for Christians these days to appreciate the power of family nurture – in Western society at least. The church has been strongly influenced by Western individualism. People are not supposed to respond to God as families or in people groups. We hear again and again that you cannot depend on the faith of your parents to save you. It has to be an individual decision.

Yet the faith of the parents should be a dynamic factor in leading the children towards Jesus. Timothy learned the faith from his

---

24. James 1:27
25. I Timothy 3:2-4 and 12
26. I Timothy 3:5

godly mother and grandmother.[27] Eunice was a believer even though her husband was not. One believing parent can bring his or her children into intergenerational blessing. Paul said to the Corinthians that the children of a Christian marriage are holy, even if only one parent is a believer.[28] Better yet, a whole family can come to Christ together. Initially, not every member may understand the nature of that decision. As time passes, each may make a genuine personal decision to follow Jesus. Our evangelism should not stop until all the family are won.

Today, however, marriages break up before or after faith. Our churches are full of single parents trying to be both father and mother. Grandparents and extended family often live too far away to be supportive. Church friends greet each other casually on Sundays, but have no meaningful contact during the week.

The church itself encourages the fragmentation of families. By adopting a graded system of Christian Education, it separates the age groups so there is no contact between the generations. Children and young people seldom mix. Teenagers believe they have nothing in common with the older generation, so they cannot even talk together. Few attempt to integrate them. It's easier to slice the church into departments and place a specialist at the head of each one.

For those of us who have never known church any other way, it is hard to realize how recent this attitude actually is. The teen-age sub-culture did not exist before the Second World War. The separation of the family in worship happened only in the 1950s and '60s, when churches began to run children's

---

27. II Timothy 1:5
28. I Corinthians 7:14

worship simultaneously with the morning service. Until then everyone went to church together. These days we have come to believe children cannot be expected to worship with their parents or to share in their spiritual lives.

WHY GOD INSISTS ON TRUSTING FAMILIES

I have asked God sometimes, "Why do you keep on expecting families to nurture their children? Even in the Bible, they did not do a very good job of it. What about the very first family? They ended in hatred and murder. Isn't there some other way to lead children to know you? Perhaps we should make our Sunday Schools better and train our teachers harder? Then when the children come out, they would all be good followers of Jesus."

But God is single-minded about his vision. He wants his children to experience family. That is the nature of the Kingdom; it is the very heart of God. The trinity is a community of three and the relationships within are familial. God has chosen to be called "Father," "Son" and "Spirit" and he wants us to share that incredible family relationship.[29] If we are to be citizens of the Kingdom, we need to learn, as a family, how to be family.

If our children can learn to honor their earthly patents and obey them, they are well equipped to honor and obey their Heavenly Father. As they learn about fathers and mothers, children are discovering what God is like. In a family, children also learn what community is like. As they do, they learn what the Kingdom of Heaven is like.

---

29. John 17:26

For too long, the church has failed to be family, and has failed to produce effective families. We have become an institution, a school, a drop-in centre. God does not intend that this should continue forever. The prophet Malachi, in talking about the end times, says,

> "He will turn the hearts of the fathers to their children, and the hearts of the children to their fathers; or else I will come and strike the land with a curse." (Mal. 4:6)

God plans to restore the family. Already we can see it happening. Organizations like Promise Keepers are beginning to blaze a trail. God's dream for children will be fulfilled. The church needs to rise up and say, "It is time we handed the nurture of our children back to the parents and families. We ourselves will be a family community especially to those children who have no spiritual family."

The prophecy does not leave us room to say, "No." If we do, God tells us clearly what will happen; our land will be cursed. Can you think of a worse curse than a generation of rebellious and lawless children?

TO THINK ABOUT

1. Tell your group how far your family has influenced your Christian life for better or worse. How far back can you trace your spiritual family tree? Write it down.

2. If you are a first generation Christian, You have the chance to start a spiritual family tree. Ask God to bless your children and grandchildren.

3. If you are a single person, ask God for spiritual children and grandchildren to become your inheritance. Where could you find them?

4. What do the children of your church learn from their experience of church life?

Chapter 3

GOD'S PLAN FOR CHILDREN. THE STRAND OF SPIRITUAL MATURITY

If family is the first strand of God's plan for children, the second strand is spiritual maturity. He does not regard them as embryo or second-class Christians. While they are still children, God gives them all they need to live a full and complete Christian life for their age.. There is nothing in the Bible to suggest they should wait until they are adults to experience the life of the Spirit.

JESUS INCLUDED CHILDREN

There were always children surrounding Jesus. They liked him. When Jesus needed a child to illustrate a spiritual truth, he did not have to go looking for one. Many were playing round the edges of the crowd. He only had to beckon and a child came running.

They had no trouble understanding him. One boy came alone to hear the preacher from Nazareth. His mother, knowing her son, had sent a good lunch to keep him going. However, he was so interested in what Jesus was saying, he forgot to eat it. When Andrew came looking for food to feed the hungry crowd,[30] the boy offered his modest meal. The people were fed, not only by the power of Jesus but also by the generosity of a child.

Jesus had a remarkable ability to speak to all generations and ages. Truth was dressed in stories, illustrations and even jokes! He did not deal in abstracts, which are inaccessible to children. He knew that if children could understand his message, it would be open to anyone who wished to receive it.

On the day Jesus entered Jerusalem in triumph, the children were there, praising and singing hosannas. This upset some religious people. They demanded that Jesus order them to be quiet, for two reasons. Firstly the children were acknowledging him as the Messiah. Surely they could not understand what they were shouting. People still say that children cannot understand worship. Secondly the children were disturbing the peace of the temple precincts.

That's the trouble with children. They like to sing and shout and raise a storm. They use their muscles as well as their minds. Apparently God likes it.[31]

Jesus reminded the rulers of the words of Psalm 8:2. "From the lips of children and infants you have ordained praise."[32]

For God, children's praise is about as perfect as it can get, because it comes from uncomplicated hearts. They do not try to find reasons, they simply appreciate him. In Psalm 148, the

---

30. John 6:8
31. Psalm 100:1
32. Matthew 21:16

Psalmist urges everyone, male and female, young and old, to praise the Lord.[33]

GOD CALLS CHILDREN

From the moment children are born, God has a vision for their lives. He calls them to serve them, and he trains them.

When he was looking for a great deliverer to lead his people out of the bondage of Egypt, he selected Moses and preserved his young life from the attacks of the enemy. When the nation was oppressed by the Philistines, God chose Samson to be the protective warrior. Before he was born, God told his parents how he should be nurtured as a Nazarite.[34]

God spoke to children at times when no one else would listen. Eli, the priest, had lost the anointing of his youth and betrayed his calling. His two sons were exploiting the worship of God for their own lust and profit. The word of the Lord was rare in Israel and there were no visions.[35] Looking for a faithful priest, God chose the boy, Samuel.[36]

His parents had a faith vision for him from birth. Even as a child, Samuel's gift of prophecy was so strong, every prophetic word he uttered was fulfilled. No wonder the whole nation came to consult Samuel about the Lord's will.[37]

When God was looking for a king, he chose a shepherd boy, the youngest of his father's house. We read that "from that

---

33. Psalm 148:12
34. Judges 13:24-25
35. I Samuel 3:1
36. I Samuel 2:35
37. I Samuel 3:19-4:1

day on the Spirit of the Lord came upon David in power."[38] It was still many years before David actually occupied the throne of Israel. He had to learn many lessons of suffering and restraint.

In Syria, an Israelite serving girl was faithful to God in spite of her loneliness and alienation. Through her testimony to the power of God, she won the greatest general of a foreign power to be a worshipper of Yahweh.[39]

God ordained Jeremiah as a prophet to the nations while he was still in the womb. When God called him, Jeremiah answered, "Ah Sovereign Lord, I do not know how to speak; I am only a child.[40]

We no longer think of children as being trainee deliverers or prophets. Two kings of Judah came to the throne as children. Joash began a huge repair and renovation program for the temple.[41] Josiah re-discovered the Book of the Law and led the nation in a great revival.[42] There seems to be no limit to what God can do with children set apart for him from their childhood.

An angel was sent to tell Zechariah and Elizabeth what God planned to with their surprise baby son, John.[43] John would be filled with the Holy Spirit. He would go before the Lord with the spirit and power of Elijah, to turn the hearts of father to

---

38. I Samuel 16:13
39. II Kings 5:15
40. Jeremiah 1:4-6
41. II Kings 12:2-5
42. II Kings 23:1-3
43. Luke 1:13-17

CHILDREN ARE EMPOWERED

If children are going to serve the Lord, they need strength beyond their own. God has no problem choosing the weak people of this world, because they know for certain they cannot do anything on their own. They need the power of the Holy Spirit.

I wonder where we gained the impression that the coming of the Holy Spirit was an adult experience? It certainly does not say so in Acts when the Spirit came on the day of Pentecost. Quoting the prophet Joel, Peter said,

> "In the last days. God says, I will pour out my Spirit on al people. Your sons and daughters will prophesy, your young men will see visions, your old men will dream dreams. Even on my servants both men and women, I will pour out my Spirit in those days and they will prophesy." (Acts 2:17-18)

Just to be sure the people got the message, Peter underlined it in verse 39.

> The promise is for you and for your children and for all who are afar off."

Clearly, the coming of the Holy Spirit was intended to be intergenerational. This idea was not original to the early church. In Old Testament times, the Spirit of God overflowed onto the children. Isaiah said,

> "I will pour out my Spirit on your offspring and my blessing on your descendants.... One will say, 'I belong to the Lord"; another will call himself by the name of Jacob; still another will write on his hand, 'The Lord's" and will take the name, Israel." (Is. 44:3-5)

Again the Lord promises,

> "My Spirit which is on you and my words which I have put in your mouth will not depart from your mouth, or from the mouths of your children, or from the mouths of their descendants from this time and forever" says the Lord. (Is 59:21)

Many people find it hard to believe that these promises are still effective in the twenty-first century after Jesus. All Christian parents hope to see their children make a salvation decision while they are young, so that whatever happens they may be assured of a place in heaven.

Yet they doubt children can receive the Holy Spirit and experience his power. I'm not sure how we can square that idea with our theology. We believe children can be saved and sometimes we are even prepared to baptize them. If our children have genuinely received Christ, they must have also received the Holy Spirit, and he is dwelling in them. (Romans 8:9)

Does the Holy Spirit remain dormant until they are old enough to reason out the theological doctrine? Not at all, for the Holy Spirit is our friend and encourager, not a doctrine to cling to. Children do not need rational arguments; intellectual problems are one of the barriers we raise to allowing the Holy Spirit to move in our lives. The gifts come without intellectual or spiritual striving, but from a relationship with God. Children know the Holy Spirit through his gentle work in their lives.

The fruit of the Spirit are the evidence of his presence in a believer's life. He can work unseen in a child's life like yeast, but it is more exciting for the child to be aware of his presence and to be co-operating with him.

Children who exercise faith can receive the Holy Spirit. Any child who can understand a personal relationship, can know him. Have you noticed how children create an invisible friend? They will talk to and love their friend until the cold adult world destroys the relationship. The imagination provides the vehicle through which the Holy Spirit can become real in the lives of young children. If they can visualize him, they can relate to him. That's why young children sometimes find it easier to relate to the Holy Spirit than older ones.

When they use their imagination, it does not mean that the things they imagine are fanciful or fictional. It simply means they can visualize things they cannot see. They cannot see a promised birthday cake but they can imagine it. On the appointed day it is real with icing and candles. So it is with the Holy Spirit. The children can imagine a vague picture of him according to the limits of their experience, but when they need him, he is there in reality.

WHAT GOD IS DOING WITH CHILDREN IN THIS GENERATION

The passage in Joel 2:28 that Peter quoted was an end-time prophecy. It was partially fulfilled on the day of Pentecost, but it will still be fulfilled as we reach the last days of the age. God is pouring out his Spirit on children in ways I have never seen before.

Around the world they are prophesying and praising, seeing visions, witnessing and leading the church in revival. I have seen children in Malaysia, The United States, in Singapore, South Africa and Argentina, who have reached out to the Holy Spirit and found him real. They love the Bible and pray with boldness.

At a conference in Malaysia, I saw children pray for a lady with a broken leg. It seemed natural that four days later she was healed and was walking about with her x-rays, praising God. At the same event there were 200 pastors and children's workers. On the last night, instead of worship and a message, Pastor Clarine Chun invited the children to pray for the delegates one by one. As they did so, simply and briefly, most of the adults fell to the ground under the power of the Spirit. Many were weeping for the children of their own churches. I watched the children seek out those leaders and hug them with the love of Jesus.

Some children regard fasting as a privilege. It is their way of telling God of their deep desires. One boy was praying and fasting for his parents. His cell leader brought the group to McDonald's for a treat. The other children urged him to eat some hamburger or fries, but he cheerfully refused. An adult, looking on, commented, "Poor boy. He can't even eat a hamburger." The boy turned and said quietly. "Please don't call me a poor kid. I'm a King's kid and I have something very important to pray for."

These children are not spiritual freaks. They are normal, enthusiastic kids, bouncy and talkative, but they have discovered that God is real and he does exciting things.

In one church in Argentina, children have a prayer ministry. They form groups of two or three and, at the pastor's request, they move about the congregation praying for adults who ask for it. On the morning when I was present, a deaf man received his hearing. This was followed by testimonies from people who had been blessed by the children's prayers during the week.

While I was in Argentina, I tripped on a loose stone and sprained my ankle. I was taken to hospital where I was told I should not set my foot on the ground for at least ten days. This was unfortunate because I was due to fly home to New Zealand in two days.

As I sat in the hotel, I received an invitation from a local children's leader to visit their ministry and see what they were doing. It was too good a chance to miss. I called a taxi and hobbled off with a friend. The meeting was in an old warehouse with bare concrete walls and no decorations. Yet the children were joyful and filled with praise.

When we were introduced, the children asked if there was something they could pray for me. I hastened to tell them about my sprained ankle so a cluster of children came forward to pray. All the other children also prayed aloud in Spanish. A leader interpreted their prayers for me. As I walked back to my seat, the pain in my ankle had gone. Back at my hotel I found the swelling was gone, though the bruising was still there. I travelled home safely and had no further trouble with my ankle.

In the United States there are children who have helped lead their church into revival. In a church in Illinois[44] the leaders were reporting to the people the mighty things that were happening during their visit to the Toronto Airport Church. As they spoke the Holy Spirit began to touch the hearts of the congregation.

In the foyer, the children were waiting to enter the church to present a Palm Sunday program. Suddenly they burst through the doors of the sanctuary and began to walk along the rows, praying for the adults. People were blessed and healed. Later one mother asked her daughter, "Why did you come into the church and pray like that? Did someone tell you to do that?" Her daughter replied, "Mom, didn't you see what happened? We saw Jesus open the door so we just followed him and did what he did.!"

I arrived in the church just after Easter and people were still being blessed and healed by the children's prayers.

Some children's leaders from Louisiana told me of an event at a children's camp. The children were being rather restless and unco-operative until at an evening meeting, the Holy Spirit came upon them in a remarkable way. They were filled with repentance and joy. Even after they had been dismissed to go to bed, they crammed themselves into one cabin and did not stop praying and praising until 3 a.m.

In Singapore children have often been moved by the Holy Spirit in their worship and cell groups. They join in prayer walks in their own neighbourhoods and some children have regular prayer walks in their schools. One boy planned to

---

44. Vineyard Fellowship, Urbana, Illinois

spend his school holidays with a group of friends, visiting classmates to tell them about Jesus.

The Esther Prayer Network for children led by Esther Ilnisky[45] reports that there are tens of thousands of children who have become worldwide prayer warriors. The G.C.W.E conference in Korea included children as delegates and they led the conference in fervent prayer for the world. At a later conference in South Africa the tent where the children were praying was filled with the Holy Spirit's wind.

In Australia, Jane Mackey lead prayer conference led by children, to empower children in other churches to pray with power.

It is hard for many churches to even conceive what God is doing with children today. If it ever happened in their church, most adults would not know what to do because they are not prepared for it. The barriers do not seem to be cultural or geographic. The main plug in the bottle seems to be the low expectations of what God can do with children when they offer themselves to Him.

TO THINK ABOUT

1. Recall some children you know. Have you ever sent them praise God with their whole heart?

2. How old were you when you were first able to take some part in the church?

---

45. The Esther Network, West Palm Springs, Florida, USA

3. Have you ever seen children receive the Holy Spirit or show some signs of his presence in their lives? Would it worry you if you did?

4. Pray that God will give you the opportunity to see him moving among the children of your church.

INTERLUDE
THE PARABLE OF THE ENEMY CONQUEROR

There was once a General, who had captured a small neighbouring country. The citizens organized strong resistance when his army first occupied their territory. Annoyed, the General called his commanders to a strategic meeting.

"I do not want to leave an occupying force in this land forever," he said. "I have other battles to fight and I wish to secure this land quickly, so that it becomes mine permanently. How can I persuade these people to accept me as their only ruler?"

One commander instantly replied: "General, I believe you should kill the chief citizens of the town. The ordinary people would have no leaders. They would then submit to your authority."

Another objected. "No, that would only harden their resistance. You should whisper false stories around the land, saying that difference factions are trying to seize the land for themselves. They would be so busy fighting each other, that they would be too weak to fight you."

A third commander nodded and smirked. "That would certainly stir up trouble but I have a better plan. It would take longer but it would *be permanently successful. Concentrate on the children. Sow discord in the families so that the children and the parents turn against each other. Teach the children that they cannot trust their parents. Teach them to ignore the older generation and to despise their ideas as old-fashioned and unscientific. Tell them that the great King who once ruled hem is no more than a myth, a legend intended to control them.*

"Make them believe our technology is the only real world there is, and there will be great rewards for those who serve it. In a generation or two they will not even know the name of their former Lord, for they will know only what you have taught them.

"Well done," said the General. "You have all spoken truth. The first plan is an immediate shock solution to remove the trouble-makers. The second is an on-going strategy, which will cripple the opposition for years. But the last plan will make this land for ever."

Chapter 4

THE SPIRITUAL BATTLE FOR CHILDREN

On a far-off day in a garden, Satan's doom was pronounced. Adam and Eve had been captured by his deception and the newly created world was now his territory. However he would not enjoy his lordship forever. God promised that one day, Satan would be forced to yield his stolen kingdom, and he would be destroyed.

Adam and Eve were forever compromised. But someday there would be a child, born of a woman, who would crush Satan and his authority.[46]

A child? Such humiliation! Of course Satan had no idea of the magnitude of God's plan: that God himself would enter childhood and win back his lost territory. Meanwhile Satan had a deep hatred for children. He still has.

Satan has sought to destroy children throughout all time, not just to make us miserable, but to protect himself. He was able to destroy Eve's immediate children by corrupting Cain to kill

---

46. Genesis 3:15

Abel. Many great leaders in the Bible – Eli, Samuel, David, Solomon – produced bad children.

Whenever Satan sensed that God was on the move, he tried to counter attack by killing the new leader before he could grow up. This happened with Moses, and again with Jesus in Bethlehem.[47] In both cases Satan was trying to frustrate a mighty act of redemption God was planning. Because he did not know which child was the special one, many children died. God rescued his future leaders through the risky actions of the adults around them.[48]

Satan has never underestimated the importance of children. To him each child is a fresh battleground, where God's will can be thwarted. He is not sentimental towards children. He sees no beauty or hope in them. They are simply targets for attack, pawns used to strike fear and terror.

Satan is also aware of the spiritual power of children. Before they have been distorted by the world, they are open to a direct approach from God in ways closed to many adults. Satan wants to shut any door by which the Holy Spirit could slip quietly into a child's life and take up residence there. If he can produce anger, fear and bitterness in a child, He can turn the child away from their Heavenly Father and His Kingdom.

In every land and culture, Satan has pursued children for evil. The ancient religions demanded the sacrifice of children, who were thrown into the flames before the image of Moloch. Children were trained to be temple prostitutes. Female or imperfect children were exposed to the elements so they would die. In Roman times a soldier away at the wars, instructed his

---

47. Matthew 2:16
48. Exodus 1:16-2:9

wife to keep their coming child if it was a boy, but to expose it if it were a girl. There was no intrinsic value in the life of a child.

Today the situation is not much better. Children are still the major sufferers in many parts of the world, even for different reasons. They die of starvation disease and exposure. There are parents who sell their girls into prostitution to keep their families alive. In some places female foetuses can be aborted at will. In some Western countries, the freedom to abort is part of the "good life." In parts of the former U.S.S.R, abortion is the only available contraception in a society in which make relatives feel they have a right to violate the young girls of their family at will.

In areas where war and poverty combine to keep people at mere survival level, children are armed to support the crimes of warlords. Often they are addicted to drugs to silence their pain. They know it is likely that they will ever grow up, so they have no qualms about taking what they want at gunpoint.

THE MUTILATION OF THE FAMILY

If family is God's plan for the nurture of children, we can be certain that Satan will try to disrupt it. He knows good Christian families can produce young people who would change the world. He would love to destroy their potential before they reach adulthood.

The easiest way is to tear families apart while the children are still young. If they experience bitterness and violence, they will reproduce it in their own families. If marriage is only a temporary arrangement, they can no longer count on a secure family environment.

Sexual or physical abuse of children is growing at an alarming rate. It is a delusional attempt to exercise power over someone weaker then oneself. Too many people believe they are helpless in the grip of the sexual urges. They do not plan to destroy children. The children are just the desirable victims of their lust.

On the other hand, so many people suspect adults of sexual abuse of children, it is hard now for a father or grandfather to show normal affection for his family. It is almost impossible for a single man to have a friendship with a child without coming under scrutiny. When a man feels that he must not touch a child for any reason at all, men will not volunteer for ministry with the children.

When children suffer, it has a profound effect on their adult lives. They carry lifelong scars of fear, blame and guilt. Among people who seek counselling as adults, many trace their pain back to the unhappiness of childhood. Their idea of God is permanently damaged. How can God be a Father to them, if their own fathers have abused or abandoned them? How can they experience the loving grace of God when they feel condemned by the world around them?

THE BREAKING OF GENERATIONAL LINES

With the breakdown of the nuclear family, extended families have almost disappeared too. Increased mobility means that many children live far away from their grandparents, not just in another city, but even on another continent.

Family relationships are restricted to Skype calls and occasional visits. For many children their grandparents, aunts, uncles and cousins are virtual strangers. The natural support of the wider family has been removed and the nuclear family has to stand alone in the world.

It is harder now for families to find support in local neighbourhoods. People move house frequently and it is not unusual for children to attend eight to ten different schools during their elementary years. Friends come and go. Few friendships, which start in childhood, last for a lifetime.

Local neighbourhoods are often just a collection of self-contained units which happen to be built in the same street. People sleep there but they use cars to go away to other places where their lives really happen. Often they barely know each other's names or talk to one another. If children cannot find community at home or in their churches, they will seek it wherever they can find it, in sports, street packs or on the internet.

Our modern youth culture is testimony to the fact that intergenerational communities have largely disappeared. Children and young people have little opportunity to talk with older people. They may know more about a computer geek who lives across the world, than they do about the old couple next door.

Every hurt, disoriented child is the founder of a new generation. Just as God plans to bless the generations of those who love him unto a thousand generations, so emerging generations may also be carrying the curse of their forebears. Sin and selfishness reproduce themselves. There is a vicious circle of pain received and pain inflicted.

Every child Satan plunders from a Christian home is a triumph for him. He is not just destroying one life. He is claiming this child's children, grandchildren and great grandchildren. That's why the church cannot be indifferent to the loss of its children. If these wounds continue in the body of Christ, the church will bleed to death.

THE RISE OF SECULARISM

If a family fails a child as a channel of nurture, the outside world will fill the gap in its own way. The dominant worldview in the twenty-first century is secular materialism. God has been removed from the agenda and replaced by self-interest and individual fulfilment. Family and community are no longer seen as a viable means of achieving satisfaction in life. A person has rights to claim and goals to achieve which supersede the rights of others.

Success is the great goal though it is measured differently in different societies. Parents who feel their own lack of success, will often try to make good through the successes of their children. For many children their personal worth is assessed, not so much by their character as by the grade o their test paper, or their victories on the sports field.

They are also a prime target for advertisers, who feed their cravings and desires. Though they have little spending power, children are enthusiastic consumers and they do not hesitate to pressure their parents for the latest "essential items". Parents, who do not have time to spend with their children, try to make up for it with presents.

Any goal which cannot be measured in material terms, is rated as secondary and optional. Our society does not mind a person being religious, so long as it does not interfere with the 'real' stuff of life, grades, popularity and image. God blends into one of many leisure options, which must not take more time or attention than the time allotted in a busy life.

Children learn these values without being taught. They know Mom and Dad are serious about education, earning their money and cleaning their teeth. If the parents see their Christian faith as something that has to be squeezed into the cracks of life their children will get the message that being a Christian is something you can do, or not do. It doesn't really matter.

Even small children understand that technology can provide most of our needs in life. Toddlers know how to turn on light or television buttons. Cars are comfortable places for sleeping. Computers can provide colourful company and infinite activities, most of which children can operate themselves. It's impossible for us to turn back the clock and live without technology. It makes for a solitary life. Real playmates are not required. Children should learn there's something better - company, friendship and commitment.

God receives little respect in our society. It is hard for people to believe in a spiritual world at all. Whereas once in a Hebrew society, God was a factor in every event of life, now we can miss him altogether. It's not that He has gone away, but we have built a world which excludes him, and that was part of Satan's plan.

The material world is so obvious and inescapable that the spiritual world feels like fantasy. There is a vast outpouring of fictional fantasy, but few people would try to base their lives on it. Most people who are attracted to the occult are attracted by the mystery and the risk, but they do not really believe in the powers they invoke. In some Asian countries where honour is paid to the spirits in popular religious ceremonies, many people believe they dealing with cultural observations rather than spiritual realities. Others would like to manipulate the spirit world to help them towards very material goals.

Children learn from early in life, that the only real things are tangible, visible and material. The things of the spirit are de-valued out of existence. It is hard to flow against the stream of the major worldview. C.S Lewis was running counter-culture when he claimed that reality lies outside the world and we live only in the 'Shadowlands'. Faith is not fantasy. It is commitment to truth.

CHILDREN'S FEELINGS ABOUT CHURCH

When children describe church, their most common word is 'boring.' In fact to them most of the ordinary world is 'boring,' but church is in a special class of its own. It is true that children are hard to entertain because they have been sated with a constant diet of slick and professional programs on television and in electronic games. Big business spends mega-dollars to attract the children's attention. How can we compete? I heard of one six-year old who was praying that Jesus would let him stay home from church!

Adults sometimes confirm the idea that church is dull. They send their children out of the service because they will not be interested. If the children are bored, perhaps some of the adults are bored too. But if God were to break through our forms of worship and touch the hearts of the people, church would not be boring. When we hear of recent answers to prayer, when people tell stories of their journey with God, when people come close to pray for each other, children can be engaged and they can participate in what God is doing.

Children should not be spectators, but active members of the worshipping community.

Of all the ugly things people said about Jesus, no one ever said he was boring. Often it's the church children who think stories about Jesus are boring. They have heard the same collection of stories repeated over and over until the life has gone out of them. Children from the non-church community get excited when they hear them for the first time. They are amazed to discover that Jesus from the Bible is still alive and touching people today.

If the church were serious about its children, we would support and equip the parents of the church, we would mobilize others in the church to become prayer partners, spiritual aunts and uncles, and grandparents. We would integrate the children into the whole life of the church and treat our children as our younger brothers and sisters in Christ.

TO THINK ABOUT

1. Do you live far away from your parents or grandparents? Do you have any extended family around you? How do you make up for the lack of family support? Grandparents, are you far away from your children and grandchildren? How can you fulfil your role in the lives of your own grandchildren and the children in your church?

2. How do children in your church feel about church? Do they feel free to worship and praise? Do they like to get involved in the mission of the church? Do they know any adults apart from their family?

3. Some of you may have experienced family breakdown yourselves. How did it affect the children? Did you have people who were able to minister to your family at the time? Pray for each other in the group.

4. If a child in your church had a serious problem, who would they be likely to talk to? Is there someone they could trust?

FLASHBACK
THE CHURCH IN THE HOUSE OF MARCELLUS

Stephen lived in a fine three-storey house, but it was not his father's. His father was a slave in the house. Dad worked for a man called, Marcellus, as a teacher for his children. Stephen's mother was a slave too. She looked after Mrs Marcellus. Stephen was a slave because his parents were slaves. He worked in the kitchens helping the cooks. Because Stephen's father was a teacher, he taught Stephen in his spare time.

Sunday was a special day in the big house. Stephen's master was a Christian as were Stephen and his parents. In the evening other Christians would come together to worship Jesus. Some of them were quite poor. Some of them were slaves or soldiers. Many would bring their children. Marcellus would provide a meal for them all.

In those days it was not safe to be a Christian. They could be caught and put in prison. When people came to the door, they had a special knock to identify themselves. If someone came who Stephen's father did not know, he would not ask if he were a Christian. He would casually scratch a picture of a fish in the sand – like this.

This was a secret code for "Jesus Christ." If the stranger recognized the picture, it meant he was a Christian. If he did not, he would not be allowed in.

As they arrived, someone would wash their feet. Sometimes it was Stephen. He would take off their sandals and clean the dust from their feet. They always smiled and thanked him, because it reminded them of how Jesus washed the feet of the disciples.

Some people brought money and gifts to share with others who did not have enough food and clothing. Stephen's mother would look after the gifts and share them out to those who needed them.

Marcellus was not the leader of the church. The leader was a man who made tents during the week. His name was Aquila and his wife was Priscilla.

When they arrived, the people greeted each other and sat down to hear what had been happening during the week. Some would tell how they had been beaten by a cruel master. Some would tell of how they had been able to tell a friend about Jesus. This was a dangerous thing to do because you could get reported to the police. Some would tell how they had had to leave their homes and hide for a while from the soldiers. Even the children would tell how they had managed to avoid worshipping idols. As they told their stories the group would praise God and thank him for helping them to be brave.

Aquila would encourage them to pray. They would thank God for his love and protection through the week. They would pray for the rulers of their town that they might be just and fair. They would pray for any of their friends who might be in prison, especially for Paul in Rome. If sick people were present, the group would lay their hands on them and place a few drops of oil on their heads. Sometimes people would be healed immediately.

After a while the group would begin to worship God. They would sing songs, sometimes from the Psalms and some new songs, which were singing praises to Jesus. People would tell stories they had heard about the things that Jesus used to do and say when he was alive. They did not have the New Testament at that time.

Some of the people would speak in a special language no one could understand, then someone else would explain what he said. One person might sense a special message that God wanted him to say to the group. Stephen liked hearing stories about Jesus. It made him feel alive and nearby. Sometimes he would feel God saying something in his heart. And he would tell the others.

Aquila would pick up a loaf of bread from the meal table, thank God for it and remember how Jesus died for them all. He would break a piece and share it around the group; everyone would have a piece. When Stephen took the bread and ate it, tears came into his eye as he thought about Jesus being nailed to a cross. He had seen people being nailed to a cross and it was horrible.

They would eat the rest of the meal and enjoy talking. When everyone had finished, Aquila would take a cup full of wine and ask God to bless it. Everyone would have a sip as it was passed around. Stephen knew the wine reminded them of the blood of Jesus which takes away our sin. He was glad he chose Jesus to be his God.

If there was a letter from Paul in prison, Priscilla would read it out because she was a good reader. After they had heard it, many people wanted to talk about it, but by this time Stephen was beginning to get sleepy. His mother would tell him to go to bed. One by one the people would slip out of the house, not all together because they didn't want to attract attention.

Chapter 5

(FOR THOSE WHO LIKE HISTORY) WHAT HAPPENED IN THE PAST

In the New Testament church children were part of God's community. They worshipped with the adults, prayed and learned with the adults. In days when many mighty acts of the Spirit were taking place, the children saw it happen before their eyes. This continued for almost three hundred years. During the years of persecution, the church continued to meet in homes in small groups.

This practice was noted by those, who opposed Christianity. In the second century A.D. a forthright critic named Celsus reported;

> "They (the Christians) get hold of the children privately, and any women who are as ignorant as themselves. Then they pour out wonderful statements. "You ought not to heed your fathers or your teachers. Obey us …. we alone know how men ought to live. If you children do as we say, you will be happy yourselves, and make your home happy."[49]

---

49. Origen, Contra Celsus 3:55, in Michael Green, Evangelism in the Early Church (Grand Rapids, Michigan: William B Eerdmans Publishing Company, 1970) 1970

Clearly the practice of including children in the meetings was still alive and healthy at that time. The complaint of Celsus was that the children were being encouraged to give up the pagan gods their father worshipped.

Children went to school for their secular education. Church leaders wanted their children to be educated so that they could be good leaders, but they learned about their faith within the shelter of their families and the house churches. Children were staunch followers of Jesus all through those years of persecution. In the catacombs there are records of children dying rather than giving up their faith in Jesus.

THE CHURCH BECAME AN INSTITUTION

Soon after the church gained official recognition, the situation changed. The next emperor after Constantine, (who had embraced Christianity,) was Julian, a short-lived emperor who tried to turn the empire back to paganism. He decreed with some logic, that because secular education was based on pagan philosophers and stories of the gods, it should not be open to Christian children.[50]

The church had to start schools for their own children. This was the beginning of a great educational institution, and it continued for a thousand years. Anyone who wanted a good education had to come to the church to receive it.

The schools were rooted in the monastic tradition. Many of the nobility could not read or write. The Christian monks had a monopoly on learning. Bible were written in Latin or Greek

---

50. Edwin A. Judge, "The interaction of Biblical and Classical Education in the Fourth Century,' Journal of Christian Education Papers 77 (July1983) 31-37.

and were hand written which made them so expensive only kings and the church could afford them. Ordinary people could only depend on the words which were read to them in Latin.

The Christian experience of children at this time was at a low ebb. Church leaders did not think it important to teach them about Jesus. So long as the children had been baptized as infants, their salvation and their place in the church was guaranteed to them. As long as they attended church, obeyed the priests and paid their dues nothing more was required of them. The clergy did all the religious work on behalf of the people.

Children learned mostly from their uneducated parents. They wer4e strictly trained in their religious duties but knew nothing of a personal relationship with God. The stained glass windows in the cathedrals were a visual aid to portray Bible truth. Occasionally travelling players might act out a Bible story in the town, but their plays were a far cry from the facts and message of the Bible. They were full of comedy, terror and wrong theology.

By the twelfth century, the wealthier merchants began to set up secular schools for their sons, breaking the monopoly of the church on education.

THE REFORMATION AND CHILDREN

The breeze of the Spirit which brought about the Reformation also touched the lives of children. Martin Luther urged his followers to teach the Bible to their children in their homes. By now the Bible was available to people cheaply in printed form and translated into their own language. Luther even wrote some hymns for them. Calvin composed some Christian instructions for children. One of his disciples, John Knox set up schools in Scotland, under the supervision of the church. The Pietist Christians of Moravia and elsewhere gave back to the children their community of faith. Count Nikolaus Zinzendorf wrote a catechism for them, intended not just to impart Biblical truth, but to lead them to love and serve Christ with their whole hearts. It was probably the world's first children's discipling book.

He encouraged them to worship and sing hymns. Regardless of their singing ability, he gathered them into small groups he called choirs. Each one had a 'kinder-vater', who was expected to earn the love and confidence of the children as he showed them how to copy the model of Jesus at their age. The kinder-vater would eventually lead them to become adults members of the church.[51]

THE CHILDREN OF REVIVAL

The sons of one outstanding family in the eighteenth century sparked off the Wesleyan Revival in England. Susannah Wesley taught her ten sons and daughters, individually to receive Christ and follow him while they were children. John and Charles were profoundly influenced by that experience.

When John Wesley began his evangelistic ministry, his care for children soon became obvious. He believed that children as young as two or three could be soundly converted and he expected to see signs of repentance and the Spirit-filled life in them. With infant mortality being rampant the urge to win children to Christ was deeply ingrained in his soul.

---

51. T.F. Kinloch, "Nikolaus Ludwig Zinzendorf" in Elmer L Towns, ed "A History of Religious Educators" 202

The children participated in small groups and for some, he set up a Christian school called Kingswood". The regime was strict but the teaching was relational. Wesley urger his teachers to say,

> "God loves you. He loves to do you good. He loves to make you happy. Would you not then love him? You love me because I love you and do you good. But it is God that makes me love you."[52]

In the United States, children were involved in the First Great Awakening. A letter written in 1705 records:

> "After a day of fasting and praying together, they first attempted to induce the heads of families to set up family worship; and God gave them great success, so that most of the families in large towns hearkened to their exhortations and reproofs; and set upon the practice of family prayer morning and evening."[53]

By 1740 when a revival was in full swing, a Mr Blair of Pennsylvania wrote:

> "There have been very comfortable instances of little children among us. Two sisters, one about seven and the other about nine years, were hopefully converted that summer, when religion was so much revived here. I (had) discourse with both lately, and

---

52. Elmer L Towns, "John Wesley" in Elmer L Towns, ed, "A History of Religious Educators," 221
53. Douglas Thorson Prayer and Revival and Reformation Societies in American History, Quoted in Intercessors for America.

from their own account and the account of their parents, there appeared to be a lasting and thorough change in them. Their parents told me that for a long time, they seemed to be almost wholly taken up with religion; that no weather through the extremity of winter would hinder them from going out daily to by-places for secret prayer, and if anything came in the way they would weep and cry. Their parents say they are very obedient children and strict observers of the Sabbath."[54]

In the mid nineteenth century, Dr Edwin Orr wrote about the Great Evangelical revival in Ireland. He recounts an incident in County Antrim:

"A schoolboy under deep conviction of sin, seemed so incapable of continuing his studies that the kindly teacher sent him home in the company of another boy. On the way home the two boys noticed an empty house and entered it to pray. At last the unhappy boy found peace, and returned immediately to his classroom to tell his teacher. "I am so happy. I have the Lord Jesus in my heart." This innocent testimony had its effect on the class, and one boy after another slipped outside. The master, standing on something to look out the window, observed the boys kneeling in prayer, each one apart, all round the school yard. Soon the whole school was in a strange disorder, and the clergyman was sent for and remained all day, dealing with peace-seekers, schoolboys, schoolgirls, teachers, parents and

---

54. Ibid

neighbors. The premises was occupied until eleven o'clock that night."[55]

The attention paid to children during the Scottish Revival began a whole new children's ministry, when their conversion was at last taken seriously.

THE RISE OF THE SUNDAY SCHOOL

The Sunday School was begun and multiplied during times of revival. Robert Raikes was a compassionate Christian whose heart was moved by the illiterate street waifs thronging the English slums. In an effort to improve their situation, he began a school to teach them to read and write. The Bible was their textbook. His concept was a radical one: every child should receive a basic education.

Schools had to be held on Sunday because in the rest of the week the children were working twelve to fourteen hours a day in mines and factories. Before long the idea caught on, and was copied across Great Britain and the United States.

Soon churches began to change the focus of the Sunday from education to Christian education and a knowledge of the Bible. By the late nineteenth century, the great Sunday School Unions were formed and denominations were encouraging all churches to form Sunday Schools. It was a tremendous advance. For the first time people were trying to teach children about Jesus in words they could understand. Dedicated people were committing their lives to serving children and leading them into a living experience of salvation.

---

55. J Edwin Orr, The Second Evangelical Awakening (London and Edinburgh: Marsha Morgan and Scott, 1955) 44.

It was a new but popular idea. In Charles Haddon Spurgeon's church in London, 8,000 children were gathered in an evangelistic rally led by the Scottish children's preacher, Payson Hammond. Some of the converts became full-time church leaders in Spurgeon's church.[56]

The children of the revivals filled the Sunday Schools and created a whole new industry producing materials and training leaders. The popular pattern was for the children to attend church with their parents, and to go to Sunday School in the afternoon. The parents were supposed to read the Sunday lessons and to support the teaching of the Sunday School in their family worship at home.

Later in the United States, the all-age Sunday School was born. Sunday School was such a success that everyone should experience it. There were classes and departments for everyone from the cradle to the grave. Christian Education became a respectable subject for seminaries, and ministers of Christian Education were appointed in churches all over the country. For years the Sunday School flourished as the spearhead of evangelism. It was the first step in planting new churches, at home or on the mission field. New converts joined and in many cases, felt more attached to their class than to their church. That was where the community and spiritual life of the church was expressed.

Some leaders tried to import the all-age Sunday School success into Australia, New Zealand and Great Britain. The transition was only briefly successful. People of reserved British stock could never feel comfortable with the idea of remaining in Sunday School for life. After a few years the all-age Sunday

---

56. Ibid 121.

Schools collapsed In most places and was replaced by the small group movement.

TO THINK ABOUT

1. How did the institution of the church exclude children from the body of Christ?

2. If you went to Sunday School at some time, do you remember what it was like? What was your best memory? What was your worst memory?

3. How many of your Sunday School friends are still Christians today?

4. Have you, or anyone you know, ever been caught up in a revival? Can you describe the atmosphere as God touches the lives of people?

Chapter 6
A CHILD'S EYE VIEW OF CHURCH

In the early twentieth century people stayed with the church because of personal relationships. It was the center of their social life. People married within the church circle and their children grew up in a close-knit society. People talked with each other and about each other. They had opinions and hobby horses. Some lived a double life. It was a small town environment, but the church was a place where people belonged together for better or worse.

That picture has almost disappeared now. People sleep in one place, work somewhere else, send their children to school at another place, and socialize wherever their car will take them. They drive to church from different communities and the children's friends at church are different from their friends at school. Many people do not mention a name when they greet people because they do not know it. They cluster round the people they know.

In this 21st century the habit of inviting people home for a meal has almost disappeared. We meet for coffee, at sports events or at restaurants. When I was a child we used to invite people home for dinner, every Sunday that we were not invited out ourselves. Eating together was part of the church culture and families got to know other families. Sometimes we would carry a packed lunch to church and spend the best part of the day together. It was called "community."

Today children do not have to leave the community of faith. Too often, there is hardly any community to leave. If the adults do not get to know each other, the children do not have any shared family contacts.

WHAT CHILDREN SEE IN CHURCH

1. The Divided Families
Children with Christian parents usually enter the church through the doors of the nursery. Sometimes they stay with their parents in the worship service. They learn that they are not supposed to talk or wriggle. If they are good they are rewarded with candies or raisins. They discover that Mom and Dad, and in fact, the whole congregation are pleased to see them there, and more pleased to see them go! A sigh of relief runs round the sanctuary when the children leave.

If they are delivered to the nursery someone cares for them. It seems pretty much like kindergarten or nursery school, except they have more songs and stories about Jesus.

Their brothers and sisters go to Sunday School in different rooms because they are older. As they grow, they too, will be promoted year after year on the basis of their school grades. This means they will forever be clustered with children of their own age. They never get to know older children or younger children nor do they meet the teenagers, adults or senior citizens of the church.

Chapter 6. A Child's Eye View of Church

The age-graded approach has been adopted by Sunday Schools in the belief that children can learn best within their own age-level. It is true that children acquire cognitive knowledge very well among their peers and according to their level of understanding. But the life of the Kingdom is more than cognitive knowledge, and spiritual truth is not grasped through our intellect alone.

Values and life-styles are better learned in a family atmosphere. For instance when a Father or mother wish to teach the children to say "please" or "thank you," can you imagine them collecting their children together in the kitchen, and giving them a notebook to write down the words and spell them correctly? Would they give them a list of situations when such words would be necessary? Would they ask the children to study the list for a test the next day, to see if they had learned the lesson?

Children learn to be polite and courteous in an atmosphere where politeness and thoughtfulness are being modelled in the family. At every opportunity they need to be reminded of what they should say. Even if the words become a habit in their conversation, the goal has not been achieved. The desired outcome of the process is that the children will become grateful, courteous people. The words are important but the heart is even more important.

So it is with the Kingdom life-style. We are aiming for transformed lives, not just religious habits. Children learn from their families and community, the heart and attitudes of Kingdom people. Parents, older brothers and sisters, aunts and uncles and grandparents are all powerful role models.

Too often the families are still being segregated at the door of the church The teens do not want the children around. The old people struggle with the teen-age music. Adults find it easier to worship without the children. The program and the pastors are mainly adult-focussed. The life of the Kingdom works in departments. Intergenerational life in the church presents huge problems to planning committees.

2. The Shallow Relationships
Usually there is a nice teacher in the Sunday School class, who will get to know the children, tell them stories and pray for them. Unfortunately, in our busy world, the teacher does not stay for long. People move about so rapidly that a year is almost long-term service.

In the earlier days, there were many devoted teachers who invested their lives in children's ministry. They are remembered with great affection by the children of their day. They visited their pupils when they were sick, and they arranged outings and picnics. They organized the celebrated Sunday School Anniversary, the social event of the year for most children, when all the girls wore new dresses and the boys tried out their worst tricks.

These days it's much harder to get teachers who can make this kind of commitment. They love the children but they don't want to lose the privilege of worshipping with the adults. They haven't time during the week for further involvement. There are few who see the ministry as a life-time commitment.

Children are quick to read what the adults are thinking. In one struggling Sunday School the children were asked to think of a new name for their Sunday School, something more modern and "hip." Amongst other names they suggested were, "Caged Kids" and "Baby Bin."

This is how many children believe that adults think about the children's ministry. It is a place where children are looked after while the serious business of ministry occurs. They will get their turn to minister one day well into the future when they have grown up. But in the meantime we put them into a holding pen.

3. Separation From the Adults

Children in a church are very aware of their size. They are small people in a roomful of adult strangers. Sometimes they know their parent's friends but they don't get to talk with them much. They are mostly waiting for their parents to decide to go home. Many adults do not know the children and do not even know which family they belong to.

Some people in the church don't want to get too close to the children. Childless couples or single adults are often shy about talking with children, because of their lack of experience. They do not feel they have any personal responsibility towards them. Older adults whose children have left home, sometimes feel they have had their turn with the children. Now they can sit back and leave it to the younger families. Yet children love to have an adult friend in the church who recognises them and talks to them.

4. There is No Sense of Awe in the Church

In some churches the children do not enter the worship service at all. They go straight to their various activities while the adults meet in the sanctuary. Over the last thirty years, people began to believe that church is far too boring for children.

One Christian Education professor told me that church for children was an inoculation against Christianity,

Church changed forever when the decision to hold the adult service at the same time as the Sunday School. Churches could plan their services without the children and except for a few occasions, church became "child-free." This arrangement simplified life for the parents on Sunday mornings They could drop off their children and sink back thankfully to enjoy the service.

When children do attend the adult service, they often regard it as a purely human activity. They are not aware that the congregation is hoping to encounter God during the worship. They do not hear the testimonies from people who have seen God working in their lives through answered prayers or miracles of healing or provision. Everything that happens is already written on the Order Sheet. There is no clue that God might be alive and present in the room.

5. Knowing is More Important than Living

Children who attend Sunday School soon learn that they are expected to know the "right answers." You get praise and respect for it. The average intelligent child can master church jargon and remember the main body of Bible stories. The ability to memorise Bible verses is also a winner in scoring achievement points. Knowing what the verses mean or how to use them it not so important. The vital thing is to get the words right.

I grew up through a thorough program of Scripture memorisation. I still thank God for that early grounding. I also grieve because for so long I didn't know how to uses the verses when I needed them. One of my earliest verses was from Psalm 56:3. I learned it from the Authorised version which read, "What time I am afraid, I will trust in Thee." At five years old I thought it meant, "What time is it when I am afraid?" A little later I discovered that it means "Whenever I am afraid I will trust in You, God" That made all the difference when I was walking home from school, feeling very afraid of the big barking dog behind the neighbour's fence.

If sharing information is the goal of our Children's Ministry, then school is an excellent model. There are hundreds of creative and well-tested methods of teaching information. Yet even at school, people often learn things they do not know how to use, nor do they have a use for them in life. Mere Bible facts and quotations do not lead to new life and spiritual maturity.

Children know that their lessons come out of a book. They are usually followed by a relevant activity. The topics tend to be predictable. 1. Children should behave well and be obedient. 2. Once long ago God used to intervene in human life with spectacular results. This teaching does not always seem very relevant in our world of technology, social media and fighting families. The world of the Bible seems very distant.

Many children in the church are afraid to ask questions or express doubts. Often leaders or parents get very uncomfortable, in case they do not have the right answers. Children often assume that the modern world is so different that adults would not understand. Teachers often discourage discussion in case they lose control of the conversation.

In a good family or children's group, talk and interruption is the name of the game. The children learn in a context of talk with topics jostling each other for attention. They will ask bold questions and defend impossible points of view. The people around them give them a context for discussion. They help them to build a basis for judgment in a world swirling with ideas.

In a child's experience, Sunday is the day for Christian teaching and it takes place in a church. From Monday to Saturday they learn about "the real world."

For many children in the church community the division is almost complete. What is true and works in church does not have much to do with their life experience outside the church.

6. How Children See the Pastor
One small boy was following his mother out of church. As she stopped to greet the preacher, he tugged at the hem of the pastor's coat. "Excuse me," he said. "You only speak to people up there, not to people now here."

Most children in the church know who the Pastor is. One child asked, "Where's God today?" when the pastor was absent for a Sunday. The Pastor is related to God and that makes him very important. They do not understand that he is also related to them. If he comes to visit their house, they are generally sent out to play. He is not part of their life and he seldom connects with them.

7. The Silence in the Homes
Many parents feel embarrassed about talking to their children about their own personal faith. Family life is a close encounter. The children are well aware that Dad or Mum sometimes lose their tempers and don't always tell the truth. Usually they forgive them because after all, no one's perfect and parents can't be "good" all the time.

But for many children their parent's experience of God is lived out behind closed doors. Do Mum and Dad pray when they are on their own? Do they depend on God when they are facing serious difficulties? Do they know how to say "Sorry,' and ask for forgiveness? Do they ever read the Bible when the children are not around?

Many children do not know how or when their parents became Christians. They haven't heard the stories of their parent's life journey, the ups and downs and the answers to prayer or perhaps the times when God did not answer their immediate prayer but cared for them another way. These stories are just as important as seeing the wedding photos.

8. Children From Outside the Church

Imagine a boy from a non-church background. Perhaps he has been to a Vacation Bible School or an Easter camp. He decides he would like to come to church to see what it is like. Would someone sit beside him to explain what is going on. Would he be allocated to a class of strange children? Would they welcome him and make him their friend?

He might enjoy the story and like the teacher, but would it mean anything in his world? Would he be allowed to ask questions? What would happen if his speech and social manners were a bit rough? Would he be invited home to visit? Would someone disciple him and lead him in the first stages of faith? Would a group of people in the church surround him, love him, pray for him and get to know his family?

If children leave our churches today before they reach adulthood, it is largely because they never see the church the way it is supposed to be. They do not see the power of God there. They never found out that they belong personally to the Christian community that God set up in their neighbourhood.

Churches want to do the best they can for their children but often they are unaware of the problems. This chapter is intended to be a mirror, so we can all see the church through the eyes of the children. In James' letter[57], we are warned about the foolish man who sees himself in the mirror and then walks away and forgets it. Confessing our problem is the first step towards repentance, and repentance is the first step towards a solution.

TO THINK ABOUT

1. What was your experience of church as a child? Do any of the reflections of this chapter chime a bell in your mind?

2. Judging by the attitudes of children you know, how do they think about the church they attend? Listen for their reactions.

3. Can you think of parents who have demonstrated the life of the Kingdom in their home?

4. Can you give a good example of a child from a non-church home, who was won and assimilated into the life of the church? How did it happen?

---

57. James1:23

Chapter 7

A CHURCH WHERE CHILDREN BELONG

What would a church look like, where the children were recognised as part of the community and where they were expected to live alongside the adults as followers of Jesus? It can happen in different models of church, but it takes attitude of understanding and family inclusion.

For some places, it seems like a natural outcome of what the church is. Where a church is based on a strong local community of families who share their daily lives with each other and express their faith together, the children are usually accepted as a matter of course. The Mennonite and Brethren communities are good examples of the church living intergenerationally.

Writers such as John Westerhoff III have argued passionately for the idea of the church living as a community of faith which included children. Elton Trueblood envisioned a "company of the committed'. Trailblazing churches such as The Church of our Savior" in Washington DC stressed the idea of community within the church which spills over into the external world. Margaret Sawin introduced 'family clusters', the gathering of families in the home for fellowship and support. In all these cases children were part of the vision.

At the same time secular schools have also been discovering the power of intergenerational groups in school through "The Peer Helpers Association" of Robert Myrick and Robert Bowman.[58] Older children are trained to befriend and assist younger ones in vertical groups.

In the midst of all this consideration, the concept of cell group church took the small group principle to its radical conclusion. The cell group became the core of the church's life. The whole life of the church flows through it.

The immediate question that arose in western churches was, "What do you do with the children and young people in a cell group church?" Could the children remain in Sunday School while the rest of the church formed cell groups? Effectively the result would be to exclude the children from the body of Christ. It would be like moving house and leaving the children to live in the old house. It is illogical to train children in a traditional church form, and then expect them to join church cells when they are teenagers or older. They need to live and breathe and grow with the cell structure while they are still children.

Suppose we were to release our old patterns of children's ministry and start with a clean page. What would we expect to see in a church where the children were part of the community?

---

58. Robert D Myrick and Robert P Bowman, Children helping Children, Minneapolis Minnesota: Educational Media Corporation, 1981

1. Family Life
They need their own families most. Parents are able to win, nurture and grow their own children. The home and the church should present a consistent model, so that children can see with their own eyes, that the things which are talked about in church are actually being practised in their own families.

2. Cell Group Life
They need a place where they belong. A cell group is such a place. Children can practise the basic life-style and service of a follower of Jesus. Other people outside the family know the children and care for them. There are other Christians to re-inforce their parent's example, and to encourage them in the victories and failures of life.

3. Celebration
Celebration is important too. As the church worships together children learn to offer their love and joy to God in praise. They need to hear the message and act on it together with their families. Worship is both celebratory and reflective. Children are well able to participate at both levels, if we prepare for them to be included.

4. Equipping Track
In the process of the family/community lifestyle, the children should be equipped to serve the Lord, just as every other Christian needs to do. It is not that they should be asked to minister in the same way that adults do. Rather they are encouraged to mature in life and ministry in the way that is appropriate for their age. Often we tend to under-estimate what children can do. Children are well able to pray for others and bless them with a word. They can listen to God for direction and guidance. They can talk naturally to their friends

AN OLD TESTAMENT EXAMPLE

When Moses first tried to lead the people of Israel out of Egypt, Pharaoh tried to water down the demand of the Lord. "Go into the desert and worship the Lord," he said, "but let it be just the men. Let the women and children stay behind."[59] God would not accept that suggestion. If the women and children did not go. Nobody would go.

Less than a year later, on the borders of the Promised Land, Moses faced the opposite problem. The spies had entered the land and brought back conflicting reports. Ten saw the fortifications and the strength of the enemy and they advised withdrawal. Joshua and Caleb said it was a good land. God had given it to them and they wanted to go forward.

When the people heard these reports, they were full of sadness and fear. They said, "If only we had died in Egypt! Or in this desert! Why is the Lord bringing us to this land only to let us fall by the sword? Our wives and children will be taken as plunder. Wouldn't it be better for us to go back to Egypt?" (Numbers 14:2-3)

Their fears for their children held them back from obeying the will of God. The Promised Land looked to them like an arena of disaster and defeat. The could only see the human outcomes – death and slavery. Even Egypt was better than that.

---

59. Exodus 10:10-11

Many people feel the same way when God challenges the church to change.

They cannot see the benefits, only the risks. They do not realise that God's promise is stronger than the obvious dangers. It is human nature to want to go back to what we know and have done before. It feels safe. But later in Numbers 14 God says to the people, "As for your children which you said would be taken as plunder, I will bring them in to enjoy the land which you have rejected. But you – your bodies will fall in the desert. Your children will be shepherds here for forty years, suffering for your unfaithfulness until the last of your bodies lies in the desert." (Numbers 14:33,33)

God intends the children to move along with the whole people of God. He does not want the people of God to hold back from his plan because of the children. If the adults of this generation turn back from the promises of God, He will fulfil His plan in the next generation.

It is never going to be easy to fully integrate our children into our churches. Our society prefers to separate them from the community. It will not be any easier in ten years' time. Must we wait another generation before we at least try to form ourselves into a Christian community?

TO THINK ABOUT

Have you ever been to a small group that loved and served one another as the early church used to do?

1. Have you ever seen children and adults integrating together in worship, or a project or in caring for one another?

2. Do you find it hard to include children in your group or in your church? Why is it hard?

3. How do the children in your church get pastored at the moment? Is it all up to the parents? What happens in a crisis? Do the children know any adults who could help?

Chapter 8

INTERGENERATIONAL CHURCH. VISIONING, PLANNING, CREATING, TRAINING

Before a church can change, it needs to receive a vision from God of what He is planning for it to be. It doesn't happen in a complete overnight transformation. The Holy Spirit stirs up a thirst for the new vision. People begin to talk about possibilities. Dreams turn into plans as the vision grows. Through prayer and discussion, the plans take shape, are adjusted, tweaked and revised. Pilot plans are tested and then tweaked again. There is the sense of the driving breath of the Spirit, drawing us onwards to new discoveries.

Cell churches need to go this process as they begin to build a new model. There is a serious temptation to work with the adults first and then bring the children into the model at a later date. It almost needs to happen that way until a sufficient base of the church has soaked in the life culture of a cell church.

The place of the children in a cell church needs to be part of the vision from the start. As the church is transforming, people need to understand that the children are also called into the cell-church community. A team of pioneers need to be planning the transformation for the children so they can begin to experience life in a group relationship.

If the children are included in the initial vision for the future church, that sets a pattern to aim for, even if it is still only at the beginning stages. We need to keep the whole vision before us, so that we don't get distracted or diverted into temporary staging posts.

THE BEGINNING OF THE JOURNEY

This happened at Faith Community Baptist Church in Singapore. When the church first became a cell church, the children were grouped in children's cell groups which met on Sunday. The groups were only loosely age-graded and the children were encouraged to relate to each other. The leaders were being trained to lead cell groups rather than "classes" and the children were learning to experience the difference.

One day at a Staff Retreat, there was a deep sense that the children were not sufficiently included in the life of the church. As we prayed, pastors testified one after another, that it was time for the children to be integrated into the cell groups in intergenerational cells. The Senior Pastor affirmed that this was his conviction from God. The church was ready to move.

The Vision for the Children needed to be written down, otherwise people might try to make changes in their own way and lead the church off-track. A written vision can give the church something which can be reviewed, to check how far the Children's Ministry is actually meeting the vision. When new leaders join the Ministry they have a clear vision statement to guide their planning. The Vision cannot be changed lightly, because it belongs to the whole church, not just to the Children's leaders.

Here is the Vision Statement for the Faith Community Baptist Church at that time.

1. All the children of the church should be integrated into the total life of the church, in outreach discipleship and service and they should grow into full Christian maturity according to their age.

2. The Children's Ministry will reach out to welcome and serve the children of Singapore by every means available in the districts and through the community services.

3. The Children's Ministry will provide quality training, internship, consultation and strategic resources for children's leaders and pastors within our church and for other churches.

4. The Children's Ministry will send children's pastors on mission teams to visit other parts of the world and to help them minister to their children.

STRATEGIES TO ACHIEVE THE VISION

When you have a vision and some specific goals, you need to set up some strategies to achieve the vision. Strategies are open to change as the situation changes. The vision remains the same. Any strategy which does not achieve the vision should be reviewed and changed. Strategies are selective and flexible.

Strategies need to be discussed by those who will need to apply them. In Faith Community Baptist Church, many strategies could not possibly be achieved without the co-operation of the parents, the cell leaders, the district pastors and the children's leaders. The Holy Spirit speaks to people in their various roles and forms a plan that everyone can support.

STRATEGIES FOR CHILDREN'S MINISTRY IN FAITH COMMUNITY BAPTIST CHURCH.

1. The Children's Ministry will support and encourage the parents of the church to become spiritual leaders to their own children and to create healthy Christian families.

2. The Children's Ministry will equip every child to be able to worship and minister in the life of the church. The children will be encouraged to share with parents in celebration whenever possible and will train for worship in their own celebration.

3. Children will be members of intergenerational cells, where they experience the life of the community, and the opportunities for shared service.

4. Children will be involved in the outreach strategies of the church in visiting, cell planting, after school clubs, harvest events and school based service.

5. Children and families who are new believers, will be received into the church through friends and family, through cell groups and if necessary, through children's leaders. The whole church should be concerned with welcoming the children.

6. Children will help form a network of prayer in their intergenerational cells, in their celebrations, in their families and among their friends, to pray blessing on the country, their schools, their neighbourhood and their church.

7. The Children's Ministry will develop the ministry skills and spiritual gifting of all the staff so that they can continue into wider ministry in the church, in the wider community of Singapore and in churches around the world.

THE PROCESS OF CHANGE

When Faith Community Church began to transition into a cell church, we started by changing the nature of the Sunday School. We re-trained all the leaders and re-grouped all the children on a wider age basis so that they could operate as cell groups for children on Sunday morning. They were real cell groups, with the ice-breaker, worship, discussion of the Word, sharing and prayer, ministry among members and a vision to reach other children.

The children responded well to this approach and they began to participate well in their groups. The leaders developed a much deeper pastoral heart towards the children. However, there were still some Biblical principles which had not been addressed.

(a) The families were still able to hand over the responsibility for the children's spiritual nurture to the children's leaders. The parents had no idea of what was happening in the children's cells and they were very willing to allow someone else to lead their children into faith.

(b) The children were still regarded as a separate department in the church. They were not seen as being part of the body. They did not experience the richness of intergenerational life – with spiritual grandparents, teenagers, aunts and uncles. Very few people in the church, outside their immediate families, could even the identify the children.

(c) The children did not have the opportunity to join in the large-scale celebration or to learn how to worship God. They did not know that their singing was supposed to bring them to meet God. Adults were afraid to invite the children into worship lest they should be a distraction.

(d) The Children's leaders were largely responsible for reaching out to community children. Yet it is often hard for them to introduce them into the church unless they have a family of their own. Parents can easily invite the children's friends into their homes and to other children's events.

(e) Children were not given any real opportunity to serve God or to minister to others. They were not expected to have any spiritual gifts. They were not trained to share their testimony or to pray for others. No one really knew how their discipleship was progressing, or even if they were facing problems in life.

Children's cell group were a big improvement on Sunday School lessons, but the children were still isolated from the body of Christ.

GOD MOVED US TO INTERGENERATIONAL CELLS

When God gave the church the vision for intergenerational cells, it was no easy change. We had to convince the cell groups that it would be good to have them there. We had to convince the parents that their children would like being there and they would behave themselves. We even had to convince children's leaders that they could trust the parents with their own children! Many of the children's leaders loved the children and had served them for a long time. They were not sure the parents would do a good job.

Before the church began to transition, the whole congregation needed to hear the vision and own it. It is not a concept that you can hear and vote on in a church members' meeting. It is a life-style which is birthed in our hearts by the Holy Spirit. If we adopt intergenerational cells as if they were another program, they will prosper briefly and then the novelty will fade, and the groups will wither.

If the church wants an "easy-fix" for its children, this is not it. People need to believe with a passion that God is saying something to them about their children. They should burn with desire to see their children as part of God's community. They will need to bear the cost and stay with the vision even when they hit rocks and potholes.

STAGES OF THE TRANSITION.

The Senior Pastor's Role
(a) Proclamation

It is essential that the Senior Pastor should be the leader of a change like this which affects everyone in the church. Our Senior Pastor at Faith Community Baptist Church, Lawrence Khong, had been one of the first to catch the vision and he was more than willing to be the spokesman. For several weeks, he shared the vision for the children through his preaching. In the districts other leaders spoke publicly about the direction we had received from God.

When introducing a change of vision and practice into the church the pastor needs to preach about it for four to six weeks. The first week the people think, "That's interesting." The second week they think, "Didn't he preach about that last Sunday?" In the third week they think, "Pastor seems serious about this." In the fourth week they think, "I wonder if God may be saying something to our church?" By the fifth week, they are thinking, "I need to pray about this." And by the sixth week they are thinking. "I'm committed. We've really got to step out in faith and see what happens."

The proclamation of the vision is a vital part of the change. If the Children's leaders begin to make the necessary changes without the covering of the Pastor's authority, the people will quickly lose heart when they discover problems. If the Pastor approves the change but never owns it personally, he will soon back down if difficulties arise. As soon as adults begin to complain, the pastor tends to withdraw and ask the children's leaders to find an easier solution.

(b) The Guardian of the Vision
Among the pastor's many responsibilities, he is the key leader in the Children's Ministry. He is not the operational leader, but he has the role of guarding the vision. If the children are not included and equipped in the church so that they drift away from the faith, he shares the responsibility. He is a guide and encourager to the children's leaders and the parents. They cannot change the vision of the church for the children, without talking to him and to the leadership.

As long as the Children's Ministry is faithfully carrying out the vision of the church they deserve the covering protection of the church leadership. The Pastor also practises his guardianship, by being in regular contact with the Children's pastor. He is encouraged by hearing of the spiritual growth of the children, and he keeps a steady course so that the vision will not go off track.

THE PILOT GROUP

At Faith Community Baptist Church, we decided to take it slowly, recognizing that not all the cell groups would be ready to accept new ideas. We needed to set up a pilot group to be our prototype, where we could make mistakes and learn from them. We could try out new ideas and keep a record of the journey for others to follow. Our Pilot group included a few future leaders of intergenerational cells so they would have experience of starting a new group.

We chose to have a two-part format. Children and adults met together in the first part of the cell meeting. The program included welcome, ice-breakers, worship and prayer for each other. Then the children would adjourn to another room while the adults were having their "Word" time. The children would also have their Word time, not just discussing God's Word but also working out how they could put it into practice. We called this session, "Kids' Slot" and the leadership was shared among the parents and willing friends of the group.

We chose a cell group where the parents really wanted to include their children. It's good to plan for success for the first experiment. Even so there were a few minor disasters. One boy fell into the swimming pool and a cell member had to jump in, fully clothed to rescue him. However, problems were a challenge to be surmounted, not a reason for closing down.

A Children's Ministry leader stayed with the group for several weeks until they felt confident. We called this stage the "Initiation." Four weeks was a good length of time to stay. If the outside leader stayed for too long the group became dependent on him/her and it slowed down the in-cell leaders.

In the first week the whole cell group met together including the children. We talked about an intergenerational cell and explained what would happen. We covered our hope and expectations, and outline how everyone was supposed to participate. We also set up a covenant relating to behaviour for both the children and the adults. (See later) We demonstrated how to include the children in the ice-breaker and the worship. We also set a person to be the Children's Co-ordinator for the cell group. This person did not have to spend all the time with the children. He or she worked alongside the Cell Leader to share responsibilities and to encourage the other members to join in.

The next week the Initiator came and led the first part of the cell group, and also the Kids Slot, with the Children's Co-ordinator and one other cell member observing. The next week the Children's Co-ordinator led the Kid's Slot with the initiator and another adult observing. The following week, one of the adult members leads the Kids' Slot with the Children's Co-ordinator observing. After that the Initiator withdrew leaving a phone number for emergencies.

Once we had one pilot group running successfully, we were able to invite members from other cell groups to come and observe. As we built up our initiating team, we were able to start more intergenerational cells. We often learned by trial and error but the results were so positive that people wanted to keep trying to improve.

Some cell groups were so impatient to become intergenerational that they would not wait for an Initiator to come to them. In almost every case these groups did not succeed. They had not prepared themselves to handle issues like discipline and control of the children. They also did not know how to run a

Kids' Slot. In most cases an Initiator was able to sort out their difficulties.

Some cell groups were so reluctant to include the children, that we left them until last. It took three years before all the cell groups who had children, became intergenerational. Even if the cell group had only one child, we still encouraged them to include that child in the group. One cell group had seven children all under two and a half years! We had to develop some special skills to help that group. Intergenerational cells are an attitude not a method. Every child needs to belong.

Some cell groups brought their children to the cell group but put them in another room and ignored them altogether while the meeting was on. This was not an acceptable alternative and we sent helpers to show them how to integrate the children.

TRAINING MEETINGS

(a) Parents

While the process was beginning, we gathered the parents together to hear their special concerns and answer their questions. We wanted to re-assure many parents who had grown up in the Sunday School themselves, and wanted their children to have a similar experience.

The most common concern was that the children would not receive consistent Bible teaching. However, when they learned that the Bible teaching on Sunday would be just as systematic, and the cell group would be used to apply the message into real life, most of them were satisfied.

Some parents vowed that they would never bring their children to the intergenerational cell group because they were afraid they would behave badly. However, in many cases they were won over when they saw what happened when their children were there. Parents discovered that their children were mostly quite normal.

Many people, who feel acutely embarrassed by their children's behaviour sometimes discover that their expectations are more rigid than they thought. They have memories of their own childhood when their parents may have been grossly restrictive. Or on the other hand, they may fear to offend the child and they tolerate behaviour which is intolerable. By watching how other families respond to their children, they often learn better ways to relate to their children.

One lady refused to bring her children to the cell group because they were hyperactive. One day she invited the cell group to her home. Her children enjoyed the cell group so much that they wanted to keep coming. Sometimes they were unco-operative, but gradually they began to change as they were accepted by the people. Their school behaviour improved too. Now she is one of the greatest promoters of intergenerational cells.

(b) Children's leaders – Sunday School teachers.

We also called together the existing children's leaders and teachers to explain the new vision to them, and to let them understand that they still had an important role in leading the children. Some of them felt very uneasy about letting the parents train their own children spiritually. One leader exclaimed, "What do the parents know about children? They're always asking us."

One young man said to our Senior Pastor, "Well, if you believe that this comes from God, we will follow you, but we certainly hope that you have got it right, because the spiritual lives of the children are at stake!"

It wasn't easy for these leaders to make the transition. They were totally committed to the children and they felt they were losing the call. Instead God was calling them into new ministries to the children. Some became worship and drama leaders for the Sunday celebration. Some of them became facilitators to the intergenerational cells. Some became leaders of the Equipping Track, systematically leading the children into spiritual maturity and service.

In a church where there are only a few cell groups, a small group of dedicated people can initiate and monitor the intergenerational cell groups. In a large church like ours, we had to train a team to be initiators and facilitators. Either way, some people have to be the trailblazers, and learn how to do it as they go.

CHURCH CHANGES FLOWING FROM INTERGENERATIONAL GROUPS

When intergenerational cells became part of the church we needed to change a surprising number of procedures to accommodate the new participation of the children. If a cell group was about to multiply, or if a new cell group was about to be formed, the local pastor needed to consult the Children's Ministry for advice on how to make the cell intergenerational.

In pastoral counselling, family problems were suddenly seen as involving the children as well as the parents. Pastors had to widen the scope of their spiritual counselling. We didn't foresee every problem that might arise. Sometimes we would look at each other and say, "What do we do with that?" Some things only became clear as we went along. God gives us vision but he does not always give us a full set of blueprints to answer all our questions.

There was very little printed material for the Kids' Slot leaders to use. We had to produce our own and train people how to develop simple ideas within their own group. Everything we learned, we passed on through the network so that other groups would hear about it.

The changes even affected the structure of the church. Under the old model, the Children's Ministry was a department on its own with a separate way of doing things. Now the Children's Ministry became a resource and advisory ministry to all the other districts of the church, and they had to think about how to integrate the children in all the other ministries.

The parents and cell group leaders and members also had a direct responsibility for the spiritual growth of the children, under the covering of the Senior Pastor. Instead of doing all the children's ministry themselves, the children leaders were often equipping others to serve the children. They also had the role of problem solving if a difficulty arose in an intergenerational cell. There was always someone to call on.

In the course of time, we discovered that local cell pastor or leaders were asking for advice in developing their intergenerational cells. They were no longer standing aloof, but wanted to know how to pastor the whole cell group. In a word, they had come to own intergenerational cells.

POSITIVE EFFECTS OF INTERGENERATIONAL CELLS.

Until they had experienced it, most adults could not believe the blessing of having the children in their company. They were humbled by the children's faith, moved by their prayers, stirred by their worship and challenged by their words. Sometimes the children asked the questions that everyone wanted to ask, but were too shy.

In most cases the children were not as unruly and disruptive as most people feared. Once the children understood that they really were part of the cell group, they responded well. However, we have had to train cell leaders. parents and helpers how to maintain good control in the cell group. (See Chapter 9)

As we built the intergenerational cells, we also learned that all the Children's Ministry needed to be co-ordinated. The life of the family, which is the smallest unit, is enriched and supported by the whole cell group. For instance the families are encouraged to pray together and to have Family Devotions/ and or Goodnight Prayers.

The Children's Sunday Celebration trains children to worship, to pray and to exercise spiritual gifts. They learn to share experiences, testify of answered prayers, share words from the Lord and care for others. The Bible teaching which takes place on Sunday often becomes the topic of the intergenerational cell. The adults respond to the Pastor's message and the children respond to the children's message. As far as possible we tried to keep the two messages flowing alongside similar themes. Families can talk to the children about the message God is directing to the whole church.

Whenever possible we liked to include the children in an intergenerational celebration service with the adults. To achieve this level of integration we had to establish good lines of communication within the church. The Senior Pastor needs to share with the Children's Ministry, the direction of the messages that God is laying on his heart.

The children's leaders need to tell the cell groups what themes are coming up so they can prepare Kid's Slot for the coming weeks. The worship leaders in the Main Celebration and in the Children's Celebration need to focus on songs which will be helpful to the children. They do not have to be "children's songs". Children can understand many simple adult songs if they are explained to them. (See Chapter 11. Worship and Celebration.) Children often understand songs better when they have accompanying actions to move their bodies.

Communication has to go in two directions: from the central Children's Ministry to the cell groups and from the cell groups back to the central Children's Ministry, all of it flowing through the senior leadership.

WHAT ABOUT THE YOUTH?

Many people want to know if young people belong to intergenerational cells too? Ideally they do. The young people make great models and mentors for the children, and they also bring a fresh dimension of thinking into the adult discussions. When the cell group enters into ministry, all the ages can co-operate across the whole community.

In a smaller church, it would be a wonderful goal, for the community of the church to be the whole community of the church. It would also give the cell group an influx of energetic young leaders who can grow up in their midst and learn the community life-style.

At Faith Community Baptist Church however, the Youth Ministry was very large and had a network of youth cells across the city. These were vigorous and committed. They penetrated the secondary schools, universities and other tertiary colleges. Some of them met in military situations, some in hospitals. They had a special field of concern and they lived by different time patterns. For this period of their lives, the church committed them to their ministry and supported their leadership. The aim was that when they completed their time of service, they would come back into the life of the regular cell groups, most of which were intergenerational.

The Children's Ministry also looked towards the Youth Ministry as the target for their emerging junior teens. The aim was that by the time of promotion, wherever possible the children would have become serious Christians who had pledged their lives to Jesus. They would have followed through basic discipleship, and be growing into spiritual maturity. They would have discovered their gifts and would be training into service to others. They would have a groups of adult mentors and be supported as they entered their teens.

When a children graduated from Children's Ministry to Youth Ministry, they were given a year to find their way in the youth cells and to get to know leaders and the breadth of the activities. In the second year they would be starting on training as Youth Cell leaders. They need to learn about youth culture and what young people can do to serve God. By the time they were fifteen, many of them were leaders or co-leaders of the junior youth cells that were clustered around secondary schools. As they graduated from school, they joined cell groups which were based in the tertiary college of their choice.

On the whole this system worked well for a long time and it still forms a workable model for city young people who are scattered over a wide pool of training opportunities. Smaller towns who lose many of their young people to the cities, would need to develop their intergenerational cells to include teenagers as well.

THE WHOLE PICTURE

An Intergenerational Church is a busy place. On Sundays the church is celebrating, sometimes in intergenerational services, sometimes in specialist services, where children are taught what worship is and how they may participate in it. The message flows on into the neighbourhood intergenerational cells, and into the specialist groups in places of work or study. As the groups apply the word of God to their lives, they begin to express their love to the community around them. They do it together with the children sharing and watching.

The cell groups work together to support outreach events or a ministry to a social need. As they grow together the children learn to live the life of Christ both by word and by demonstration.

TO THINK ABOUT

1. What advantages can you see in having the whole family sharing in the cell group?

2. What are the points which might be a struggle for you?

3. How does your church help parents to lead their families in spiritual worship and in daily life?

4. Is there any meaningful way you could include some of your children in the main worship service? How would the adults have to change their thinking?

INTERLUDE

THE INTERGENERATIONAL EXPERIENCE

Angela was ready to open the door almost before the doorbell rang. She was excited because the cell group was visiting her home that night. She'd even tidied her bedroom so the children could have room for Kids' Slot.

It took half an hour before the whole cell group had arrived. Angela's friend, Lucy, came early and the two girls rushed off to get ready for the icebreaker they had prepared. They kept it a secret until the cell leader invited them to start the cell group.

Lucy gave each person a piece of paper and a pencil while Angela told everyone to draw a picture of themselves. In a few minutes she collected the folded drawings and put them in a basket. Then she asked them all to take a drawing at random. Each person had to decide who the drawing represented and write the name of that person on the paper. There was a lot of laughter as people made wrong guesses. Even little Sharon joined in because her Dad helped her.

Uncle Barry was leading the worship. Angela liked the worship. It felt good to be close to God, singing songs to Him. Matthew like to be the one who managed the visuals. Sharon shook the bells and Paul played the tambourine. Robert who was two years older than Angela, started dong "sign language." Angela and Lucy were quick to join in. Uncle

Barry suggested that they should all try to learn the signs. Angela was surprised to see how well her Mum picked them up. Old Aunty Edith and Uncle George tried very hard but they kept getting mixed up. Still they loved to sing.

When the cell leader asked the group if they had a special verse from the Bible to share, Robert read a verse from his daily reading. "I can do all things through Christ who strengthens me." Angela silently decided that she must start reading her Bible again like Robert.

Later when the cell leader asked if anyone had heard God speaking to them this week, Angela remembered the verse she had learned last Sunday at celebration. She said, "God says that we should cast our worries on Him because He cares for us."

"That's good, Angela", said the cell leader. Then Angela noticed a tear sparkling in her mother's eye. There was a pause.

"I just want to tell you," said Mum, "that the Lord spoke to me just now through Angela. I've been feeling so miserable today. I've had bad toothache and it's made me so cross with the children. But I can't afford to go to the dentist just now. Would you pray for me?"

So the cell group gathered around Angela's Mum and several people prayed for her and her tooth. Angela prayed too.

"Do any of the children have something special they would like to pray about?" asked the cell leader.

Robert raised his hand. I have important school tests next Wednesday. I'd like you to pray for that."

"I have tests too," offered Sharon who had just entered kindergarten.

Matthew was looking uncomfortable. "I have this teacher at school who doesn't seem to like me very much. I mean he always seems to blame me when things go wrong. Wouldn't hurt to pray about it, I guess."

So they did.

Auntie Tina was leading the Kids' Slot that night so the children followed her into Angela's bedroom. Everyone sat in a circle and Aunty Tina started a clapping game. You had to say everyone's name without losing the rhythm. Angela was surprised at how hard it was.

Aunty Tina reminded Angela of the Bible verse she had quoted earlier. "That was a great verse you learn on Sunday. What was the Bible story that went with it?"

"It was about that lady who didn't have enough food for her little boy, and then Elijah came along and asked her for a cake. And she made on for him even though it was the last food she had.'

"So what happened then,?" asked Aunty Tina.

"Well, next day there was enough flour and oil for another cake, and then another cake and then another one the next day. And that went on every day until there was enough for everyone again."

'And the little boy didn't have any food," added Sharon sadly.

"Afterwards he did", replied Paul. "After Elijah came along."

"So why did you have that memory verse?" asked Aunty Tina.

There was a pause. Paul spoke up again. "Well, when we haven't got enough food, we should talk to God and He'll give us some."

"No, it's more than that," added Robert. "It's not just food. Pastor said in church that God will look after anything that's worrying us, if we tell Him about it." Isn't that right, Aunty Tina?"

"Yes, that's right, Robert. Doesn't always happen straight away though. Two months ago my car broke down and I didn't have enough money to fix it. It was very hard for me to get to work by bus. But last week I had a surprise letter from the Tax Department. They said they had charged me too much money and they were sending some back to me. I was so amazed. It was just enough to pay for my car repairs."

"Does that mean that God will fix Angela's Mum's toothache?" asked Lucy.

"I hope so," sighed Angela. "She gets so crabby when her tooth is sore."

"Why don't we act out the story of Elijah and the widow lady?" suggested Aunty Tina.

So they did. Robert was Elijah and Angela was the widow and Paul was the widow's son. Then they did it again with Lucy as the widow and Matthew as Elijah. Sharon wanted to be the widow's son because, "Poor boy, he didn't have enough to eat."

After they'd finished acting and laughing, Aunty Tina said, "Let's open our notebooks and see what we planned to do last week." Oh, last week you planned to put aside ten percent of your pocket money to give to God. Did any of you remember?"

"I did," said Paul eagerly. "I remembered as soon as I got my pocket-money. I put fifty cents in this envelope to put in the offering.

"I forgot," said Angela, "until Lucy reminded me and then it was too late."

Same here," admitted Robert, "but I'll put double aside this week."

Interlude. The Intergenerational Experience

"I asked Dad for pocket money and he gave me 20 cents," said Sharon.

"So how much money do I need to give?"

Aunty Tina smiled. "Two cents, Sharon, and if you save it up for a little while you'll have ten cents to give." "So what do you think God wants us to do about his word to us this week?"

Sharon jumped in. "We should give some food to any boys who haven't got enough to eat."

They all smiled, but then Robert added, "She's right, you know. We're so lucky and some kids really go to bed hungry. Let's pray for them every day this week."

"O.K that's a good idea. Write in into the notebook Angela. We'll ask each other next week if we remembered."

"I think we should do more than that," added Lucy. "I think we should collect our money next week and give it to children in the world who are hungry."

"What do the rest of you think about that?' asked Aunty Tina.

Yeah, we could do that," nodded Robert and the others agreed.

"Would you like to ask the adults to join in?" asked Aunty Tina.

"They can if they like, said Angela, but it's our offering."

"Please, I've got a problem, said Lucy. "There's a girl in my school who writes nasty notes about me and passes them round the class. I hate her. I don't even want to go to school."

"Oh dear, that sounds very miserable, Lucy. We'd better tell Jesus about it. He knows why she's doing it and he might be able to stop her. Do you think she might want to come to one of our cell group outings one day?"

Lucy shook her head. "I don't think so. She laughs at me all the time."

"Well let's try anyway."

So Angela prayed for Lucy and the girl at school and everyone held hands around Lucy.

"Can we pray for Mum's toothache too?" asked Angela. So they prayed again and wrote it down in their notebook.

By now it was time to go back to the adults. They staged their little play all over again and the adults enjoyed it.

Aunty Tina said, "I have a surprise here." She went to the kitchen and came back with a beautiful cake with all the candles alight. "This is for Uncle George. He was 79 years old yesterday."

Uncle George broke into a wide smile. "So good of you. I never expected this."

Aunty Tina started singing "Happy Birthday," and everyone joined in. Soon they were all munching cake and trying not to spill the crumbs on the floor.

It was time to go home Everyone hugged Uncle George again and said good-bye to one another. The cell group was over.

Mum's tooth settled down that night so she could sleep. Later in the week Mum received a letter. It contained two hundred dollars. "This is to help you go to the dentist," the letter read, "with love from your cell group."

Chapter 9

LEARNING TO OPERATE INTERGENERATIONAL CELLS

Intergenerational church did not begin in Singapore. The idea of an integrated Christian community has been an ideal right from the New Testament until now and in many different cultures and societies. In pioneer rural settlements it was normal to include the children. In places where Christians were breaking away from the traditions and standards of the official church, the children were swept along in the movements of the radical church.

Amish and Mennonite communities always included their children. The Plymouth Brethren fellowships of my childhood did not see themselves as churches but as a "little flock" which included everyone. It may not have been up-market, but it was the place where we belonged.

In more recent experiments in community church the same mindset has emerged. The house churches in Canberra, Australia, under the leadership of Dr Robert Banks, had their "church" service on Friday night so that all the children could participate. Some nights they focussed more on the children.

Some nights the children's participation was low-key, so that the adults could discuss adult-life issues.

In Latin American churches it was not possible or desirable to exclude the children so people had to get used to having the children with them. At times the need for cell group leaders was so great that older children and early teens had to be trained to lead groups. They earned the respect of the adults and helped the groups to grow effectively.

The intergenerational concept did not always result in the same structures. People prayed and experimented and listened to the Holy Spirit and modified their model. The great overall outcome was that in these churches there was no barrier between age-groups in the congregation.

The Intergenerational cell groups I describe in this chapter, happened at Faith Community Baptist Church over the ten years I was acting as Staff Consultant. It was a huge opportunity and blessing to me, because of the graciousness and trust of the Senior Pastor and the Church leadership, who gave me to the permission and the space to do something new and practical within the vision that the Holy Spirit had birthed in me.

PRACTISING INTERGENERATIONAL CELLS WITH CHILDREN

When we started operating intergenerational cells, some things worked out quite easily. The children loved being part of the activity and often they came up with excellent icebreaker ideas. Even the little ones could participate if they could partner with an older child or adult.

The worship was not much of a problem either. We encouraged cell groups to buy or make percussion instruments to accompany the music. Some children who were learning music were asked to bring their instruments if possible and to use their gifts in leading the group in worship. Children who were coming to the cell group for the first time, understood very quickly what worship was about, especially when the leaders took time to explain to them what was happening. The freshness and spontaneity of the children often revitalised the adult worship. Before long children were helping to choose worship songs. When the leader asked if anyone had a word from the Lord, the children began to also take courage and speak up what they knew.

Having the children present during the prayer time also "caught on" quickly. It wasn't long before the children understood that when a person was sick or had a need, the normal thing to do, was to pray for them. I remember one four-year-old entering the cell group one evening. He saw a young "uncle" with his leg in a plaster cast and propped up on a stool. His immediate reaction was to run across and lay his hands on the plaster cast, and to call out, "Pway, Pway!"

Sometime adults struggled to be open enough to let the children pray for them. One week a man in the group asked for prayer for his new business which had only just started. A boy in the group took up the challenge and prayed for that man and his business every day that week. Next cell meeting, he ran up to the man and asked, "How did your business go this week?"

The man just smiled and said, "Fine, fine". However, a little later the boy heard the man confess to another adult that it had been a tough week, and he didn't know it was going to work out.

On the way home the boy said to his father, "Why couldn't Mr Brown have told me that? I only wanted to pray for him."

Adults feel very vulnerable when children offer to pray for them. They feel it should be the other way round and it takes a while before they are humble enough to tell the children that they have needs. Sometimes the children are the ones to be embarrassed. It is hard to talk about problems at school when Mum and Dad are present. It takes a little while for an atmosphere of trust to develop in the group.

The group tried to notice special events in the life of the families- birthdays, new babies, new jobs, achievements, and disappointments.

When the time came for the group to respond to the Word of God, (which was often a follow-up on Sunday's message), the group divided into sub-groups. The adults often preferred to talk about the Word and the children preferred to review and respond to the Word.

We called the children's group, "Kids' Slot." They moved to another room in the house and were led by an older person. It did not have to be the same person every time. The children were quite happy to have a different adult each time and it helped them to get to know the adults. Some of the men tried to leave that role to the women of the group, but we encouraged them to take part and we showed them how to do it. Children really appreciate getting to know and learn from men. In their educational experience, they are often surrounded by women for up to eight years of their early education. Boys like to get

Chapter 9. Learning to Operate Intergenerational Cells   129

to know and respect men they can trust. They love to have a life hero to follow. It's all part of being family. Sometimes we had an assistant to help the leader to protect the group from vulnerability and security issues.

After about forty-five minutes the two groups came back together to report what they had done. Often the group shared some food at the same time. Each group told the other group what they have been doing. In some groups there were people who could put together a program outline for the Kids' Slot. At Faith Community Baptist Church, we had so many intergenerational cells that we had a children's leader to put together a Kid's Slot each week and to email it to the cell leaders. We were able to train some of leaders to specialize in this ministry. We kept the format fairly easy and predictable to help people who had not experienced children's ministry.

OBSTACLES THAT OFTEN ARISE

(a) Behavior

When we first began talking about intergenerational cells, the first questions that arose was, "How will we make the children behave?" Some parents shuddered when they thought of the disturbance their children could create. They would rather stay away than be embarrassed by their child. It was especially hard for single parents who normally paid for a baby sitter or had to stay home from the cell group. Some older people and single people had little contact with children, and they feared the cell group would become very disruptive.

At the very first initiation meeting the whole group, including the children, talked about the behaviour standards would are acceptable in a cell group. We discussed a Group Agreement which set out the way the members of the cell group should behave towards each other. The agreement was not one-sided. It included both children and adults. Many of the suggestions came from the group. We should show respect to each other but waiting for our turn to speak. We should be polite and listen to what other people say. We should honour each other's privacy and not embarrass other people by telling things about them without their permission. Children also need to ask their parents before they tell about family conversations.

For some children, this was their first visit to a home which does not belong to a relative. They did not know how to behave so the cell group was a good place to learn. We composed a set of House Rules about how the Hosts would like us to behave in their home. Everyone, including the children, contributed good ideas. It is polite for the group members to take off their shoes. The children understand that they may not run or jump inside. They should not use equipment without permission. They may not bounce on beds or on other furniture. They may not write on the walls or the carpet. That may seem unnecessary but we discovered that it's best to say it.

The children are shown how to use the bathroom; how to use the taps and turn them off; which towels they should use. The group should never allow two children to go to the bathroom at the same time unless an older child is helping a younger one. The children should not help themselves to food unless they have been invited, and they should try to serve other people first.

Generally, we expect parents to deal with discipline problems but if they are not aware of unacceptable behaviour, another adult, especially the cell leader, may explain why there is a problem. Often just a word or a look from another cell member is enough. Spiritual grandparents can be such a blessing in a group. If a mother has been caring for two lively toddlers all day, she needs a break in the cell group. Children respond very well to an elderly friend who cares for them. It is a service of love to the family.

Most children want to be part of the cell group. They think it is a privilege to be members. If they are reluctant to come to the group, it is often because they feel isolated or left out. Once they are recognised and included as members of the group, they begin to recognise the adults and to care for them.

It is not only the children who can misbehave in a cell group. In one of our early groups the adults had a loud argument which ended in anger and tears. The children were unwilling witnesses to this upsetting event. It could easily have closed the cell group. During the week the cell leader talked to the adults who had been involved. By that time, they were beginning to feel embarrassed and a bit ashamed. Next week the cell leader explained that the adults had had a disagreement last week, but that didn't mean they were not friends anymore. They were very sorry for the bad things they had said and they were even more sorry that they had been a bad example of what a Christian is. The children accepted that they were not perfect and forgave them for the incident. It was a good example that all of us can do wrong things and all of us can be forgiven.

(b) Age Differences

People who have been accustomed to Sunday School, find it alarming to have children of different ages in the one group. They cannot imagine how to keep the attention of a three-year-old and an eleven-year-old. If you are trying to teach the children information, it is a real problem. If you are trying to build them into a family, it is very different. Some people have tried to turn the Kids' Slot into a Sunday School lesson. That is, they want the children to sit quietly while they teach them a lesson. If the children have been to a celebration, they will have already had one teaching message on Sunday. The aim of the Kids' Slot is to explore the message further and work out what it means in practical life. The Kids' Slot is usually made up of conversation, role plays, personal stories on the same theme. They can talk about how similar situations work out at school, and ask questions about problem areas. They will revise their memory verses and think of situations when they would be useful.

Often there may be a craft or activity which illustrates the point of the message, or they may plan an action which gives them a chance to obey the message God has given them. There might be a game which illustrates the idea they have heard. The older children and the younger ones participate according to their age, or in partners when they can help each other. Games are never a waste of time in a cell group. They are a great opportunity to learn relational and negotiating skills. Younger children will often ignore the rules and play with great enthusiasm and little understanding. Junior children play with great attention to the rules and will spend more time arguing about the rules than playing the game. Older children will bend the rule to reach a desired outcome. "Let little James move his counter. He likes it there and it doesn't matter if more than one person wins." This is how groups bond together.

An important part of the Kids' Slot is the ministry time, when the children pray for each other and ask God to bless them in their various schools or situations. They may learn to call upon the help of the Holy Spirit when they are in difficult situations and to have some Bible verses they can remember.

The children can be concerned about children in other parts of the world, to understand their life-style and to learn how God can help them. Collections and scrapbooks can be an effective way of enlarging their knowledge. At one time I challenged a group of intergenerational children to learn the books of the Bible, just to see if they could. They tried very hard and all of them succeeded to some extent. The youngest one who completed the task was five years old!

(c) Including the Younger Children.
Intergenerational groups seem to have one great advantage. Children everywhere seem to have an in-built concern for children who are a year or two younger than themselves. They do not feel the same way towards children of their own age. Among their peers they are striving to show they are equal to all the others, and preferably a bit better. If one child tries out a stupid trick, every other child has to do it just to show they can.

However, if a child is obviously younger and less able to do things, children like to help and show them what to do. Even a five-year-old likes to help a three-year-old. When we first started intergenerational cells at Faith Community Baptist Church, we said that children three years old and under were not allowed to go to the Kids' Slot but had to stay with their parents. Often younger children were put down for a sleep. To our surprise the three-year olds quickly told us they wanted to be with the "big kids". When we asked the older children if they minded, they were usually happy to include them.

If the younger children are present in the Kids' Slot, they are sure to lose interest sometimes and start doing something else. They have a very short attention span. That's not a disaster. They can do some new little task and be praised for it. They do not have to focus attention all the time. In some groups there were so many very young children that there was not attempt to involve them in a formal program. They used songs and little games with rhythm. They were still forming relationships and felt part of the family.

Occasionally mature older children have wanted to stay with the adults. This can be a good experience for them if the adults feel comfortable with that. Yet the older children also have an excellent role in being leaders and role models for the younger ones.

(d) Leadership of the Kids' Slot
A few people in the cell group want to lead the Kids' Slot all the time but this is not a good idea. They often miss out on the ministry and fellowship of the adults in the group. Sometimes they feel safer with the children. Some people would rather not be with the children at all. They don't feel they have the skills to get close to children. Yet every member of the cell had something valuable to share with the children. The children also have a fresh blessing ro share with us.

At first some people will not feel able to lead the Kids' Slot on their own. People can lead the children in pairs, husbands and wives, adults and young people. Many new leaders blossom into enthusiasm when they discover that the children like to be with them. A man in my own cell group felt totally out of his depth in talking with the children, but finally he paired up with me to give it a try. After that he was always keen to take his turn and he was a very popular leader.

Most new leaders need to learn a few basic things about how to control a group of children. About every three months the church had an evening class when adults could gather some new skills about interacting with children.

Every member of the cell group is expected to relate to the children in some way during the cell group. For elderly people it may be sitting next to a child and having a conversation with them. We liked to give the older people a chance to tell stories about how things were years ago when they were young.

Sometimes we would encourage cell members to tell the children somethings about themselves. It could be about their work, or a hobby or sport or a funny experience, or practically anything that is a new idea to the children. As the children find out how the adults live, they are also discovering that Christians come from all kinds of backgrounds and experience.

Many children have a very narrow idea of what a Christian is. They are people who come to church. It is a revelation to them to discover their cell friend is a champion weightlifter or that he works as a stuntman in the movies. Imagine that! Anyone can be a follower of Jesus.

(e) Space and Time

In many Asian churches the apartments are very small without yards or gardens for the children, so they have to be creative about making room for the children. In one case there were two cell families living in the same building, so the children could adjourn to another apartment. Sometimes the family will stack the beds in one room to create some space, or they have asked permission to use a space under the building or in the lobby.

In other countries I have seen children meet in gardens, garages or in basements. In one group there were more children than adults, so the children stayed in the living room while the adults adjourned to the bedroom.

Many parents are concerned about bringing their children to the cell group because of the late hour at which the meeting ends. Friday night is a popular night for cell groups because the children do not have to go to school the next day. In Singapore children usually stay up quite late at night so it is acceptable for the cell group to end at 10.30 p.m.

In other western countries however children go to bed much earlier so people have to make a different plan. In Australia the cell groups would meet as soon as they can after work, and they would share a "pot-luck" dinner. Their aim was to finish the cell group at 8.30 pm. Other groups have chosen to meet on a Saturday or late on a Sunday afternoon.

At some stage the group needs to discuss time and place to work out a solution that will work best for them. If the group decides on a finishing time, the leader must actually end the group at that time. In that way, any parents who wish to take their children home are free to do so without feeling embarrassed.

The Kids' Slot should not take more than about 40-45 minutes. The adults need to know when they can expect the children to come back. There needs to be time for reporting back, for food, for "Good-bye" prayers etc.

If a deep pastoral problem arises in the adult group, the cell leader should arrange another time for some of the group to meet to talk about it.

(f) Multiplication of Intergenerational Cells

When a cell group is ready to multiply, the children need to be involved in the change. Everyone in the group should know from the beginning that the aim of the group is to grow large enough to become two groups. Yet when the time comes it is hard to separate from their friends. Usually we will try to keep close friends together especially people who may be sponsoring each other. The parents talk with the children and they pray together about which new cell group they should join. We found in practice that the children were generally very adaptable and soon learned to be happy in their new cell group.

Sometimes there are not enough children in the group for both new groups to be intergenerational. People are often sad about that, since neither group wants to lose the children. Sometimes you can do a three-way multiplication so that the children can be spread over three groups.

If a cell group has more young children than adults, it is hard to function as an intergenerational cell group. It takes all the efforts of the adults to support the children and the group tends to revert to a children's cell group. It is hard for such a cell group to multiply. New families or adults find themselves a bit overwhelmed by the children.

If a cell group is having an outreach towards their children's friends, or the children from the local community, the number of children in the cell group can increase rapidly. Sometimes it is necessary to form a satellite cell group to disciple children who are just coming into faith. This should be regarded as a ministry of the mother cell and led by some cell group members.

The cell members are also responsible for meeting the parents of these children. The final aim is that the children bring their parents into the cell group and become fully intergenerational again.

In healthy intergenerational cell groups, there need to be a balance between adults, young people and children. The children should not be the dominant factor. This is a thought we need to consider when planning for a cell multiplication.

(g) Some Blessings We Didn't Expect

We never ceased to be amazed at the good things God has done through the intergenerational cells. Some people worried that single people would feel excluded. In many cases they were some of our most enthusiastic leaders. One group was made up entirely of single adults, but they chose to become an intergenerational cell. They gathered nieces and nephews and children from the locality to form an intergenerational community.

Sometimes when the cell groups were in apartment buildings, other children in neighbouring apartments thought that the children seemed to be having fun, so they asked if they could join in.

We were delighted with the enthusiasm of the children. Two boys had parents who were often out of town on business. When they were away the boys insisted on being sent to the cell group by taxi.

As the cell groups have moved about the neighbourhood visiting different homes, we have discovered some children whose parents were reluctant to bring to their children to the Sunday celebration. When the children discovered what happens in the cell group, they suddenly wanted to come on Sunday too.

The presence of the children undoubtedly lifted the level of the adult worship. The children are very direct and receptive to the styles of worship. They are not afraid to move rhythmically or to use actions. They are quick to respond when they are invited to share a prayer or a word. They like to take a turn in leading the worship themselves and sometimes they will teach the adults a new song.

One of the most wonderful things in the intergenerational cell groups has been the joy of the parents in sharing with their children. It seemed more natural to talk with the children about spiritual things and the habit of praying for each other, especially in time of difficulties, just flowed through into the families. It also helped single parents to have some safe men who could mentor their children.

IS IT WORTH THE EFFORT OF THE CHANGE?

No-one can pretend that introducing intergenerational cells is an easy choice. It takes commitment from almost everyone in the church. People need to learn what an intergenerational cell is like and where the children belong in the church. Many churches can see the benefits of intergenerational cells, but cannot face the struggle of change.

Whenever you decide to introduce intergenerational cells it will be hard. People hate moving out their cell church comfort zone. They need to hear Biblical teaching on how God regards children within the church family, and how the

New Testament church contained the children in a vibrant Christian community. Sometimes the vision process takes a while until the parents and congregation begin to feel hungry for the spiritual growth of their children.

During this time plans can be made, people can be trained and pilot groups can be tested. But the church cannot wait for the last laggard to come on board. Some people take longer to process things. It is never going to be easier than it is now. As the movement begins to gain momentum more people will want to try it out. The most important prerequisite is a firm call from the Lord to the church for the children. Without that, it will only be a flimsy structure. Change is not based on curiosity but on conviction.

TO THINK ABOUT

1. What might cause the parents to feel uncomfortable about bringing their children to cell group?

2. What training would cell members need to be able to take a turn in leading Kids' Slot?

3. How would you encourage single adults and elderly people to enjoy an intergenerational cell group.

Chapter 10

CHILDREN'S CELL GROUPS. A STEPPING STONE TO INTERGENERATIONAL CELLS

Often people get excited about intergenerational church or cell groups, but it is not possible to make a transition just yet. The leadership of the church may not have caught the vision just or the congregation may not be ready for change. People need to start talking and dreaming, beginning to feel the fractures of the present system. Everyone in the church wants the children to come to faith and to mature into leadership. They only begin to worry when they can see that the process is not happening, and that they are losing the younger generation.

In the meantime, the Children's Ministry can begin to develop children's cell groups on a Sunday, to create a relational model which will help the children feel that they have a place to belong. Sunday cell groups are usually adult-led but in a context of mutual discussion, ministry to each other, and spiritual growth. They do not have to be age-graded but the older ones are given leadership responsibilities. Often the children will be given partners or buddies to take special care of each other.

In some large churches, the Bible teaching is given by skilled communicators or a team who can engage the children effectively. This may be supported by drama, games, exercises, memory verses and testimonies.

When the children separate into the cell groups, the aim of the group is to apply the message, to minister to the needs of the children, to help the children to minister to each other, to learn to pray for each other, to strengthen each other for the week ahead, and to plan for external activities. They may be social or skill based, (e.g. kite-flying, sports, outings). They may include other friends from school or the neighbourhood. They may join an adult event such as prayer-walking. The group becomes a mini-community where the children find friendship, safety and discipleship.

One excellent model of children's cell group was operating in the Shepherd Community Church in HongKong, pastored by Dr Ben Wong. The children met in a large open area in the same building as the adult congregation. The worship and message was led by a trained leader and a worship team, and lasted almost an hour.

Then the children's congregation broke up into mixed-age groups scattered around the available area. Each group had two older children leading the group, one was the leader, and one, the co-leader. The co-leader was training to take over the leadership next year. There was also an adult attached to the group but he/she was not the leader but the support person. If there was a problem of behaviour or any other difficulty the adult was a resource person.

Chapter 10. Children's Cell Groups.
A Stepping Stone to Intergenerational Cells

The group would begin with a game or ice-breaker and then the leader reviewed the message they had just heard, asking and answering any questions and making sure the children understood. They would work out how the message could be applied at home or school. Often they would recall last week's memory verse or introduce a new one. They would end the group by praying for one another and sharing any needs.

By that time the adult congregation was emerging, so the children joined their families. However, the group-leaders and the staff leaders stayed back for a de-briefing of the group session and a preparation for next week's program. After that they adjourned to McDonald's for some fun and friendship together.

This was an excellent model for children's cell groups because the children were being equipped for maturity and leadership. The younger children related well to their group leaders and looked up to them with respect.

CLASS OR CELL-GROUP?

When the Children's Ministry transitions from a Sunday School class to a cell group, the old leaders find it hard to learn the new relational culture. Even after initial training, we found leaders would lapse back into being teachers so that we had to run refresher training about once a month. People who have been used to doing all the talking while the children listen, do not feel comfortable with opening up the conversation for the children to share. We tried to help them see the family as their cultural model rather than the school.

In one church which was experimenting with children's cell groups, all the groups were mixed ages, except for one. A group of 11-12 year old girls rebelled and complained to their parents so that, in the end, they were allowed to keep their social group. This was the only group which had discipline problems. It was also the one in which there were fewer signs of spiritual growth. It was designed for selfish reasons and it produced selfish results.

LOOKING TO THE FUTURE

If children learn the character of a cell group before they try to integrate into an intergenerational cell group, the transition is much easier. They already know about sharing needs and praying for one another. Hopefully they will be developing a concern for their friends who don't know about Jesus. They will also have started on the journey into discipleship so they know what an active Christian life looks like.

The main disadvantage of children's cell groups is that the children are still isolated from the parents in their church and spiritual life. The parents do not get so much opportunity see how their children are growing and to lead them in practising the Christian life as a family.

As long as the children are separated from the main-stream ministry of the church, they do not know what the church does, how it operates or how they can be part of it. The church can run an Equipping Track for the children but they do not give them the opportunity to practise it with other adults and especially their parents.

The longer you have an Intergenerational Church, the more you can see its benefits. It takes time to see the children maturing, trying out the skills and learning to trust the adults around them. Families report more positive communication and encouragement among the children and the adults.

TO THINK ABOUT

1. What sort of change would it take to convert our Sunday School into children's cell groups?

2. Would this be a good means of preparing the children for Intergenerational Cell Groups in the future?

3. Would children's cell groups fulfil the vision of our church for the children and the families?

Chapter 11
WORSHIP AND CELEBRATION

Timothy sat in church waiting for it to be over. Funny how this hour of the week seemed like a whole year, when other hours were just a few minutes. He cheered up a bit when the pastor said "Finally..." but it was still another seven minutes before he stopped. Timothy timed it on his watch. He usually did.

Then the music began again, and the people started worshipping. How could adults actually enjoy worshipping? They sang the same old songs over and over. Some of them raised their arms and closed their eyes, so it looked as if they were off the planet. It was embarrassing. Timothy couldn't believe that he would ever enjoy worshipping when he grew up.

Timothy never stood up for worship. If he did he might be expected to join in, so he sat slumped in his seat. He wishes he could get out his electronic game. But his parents would never allow that. He just had to sit and suffer. Surely it couldn't go on much longer. His tummy was reminding him it was dinner time. He was beginning to think he was in a time warp where church would go on for ever. He wondered if this is what Heaven would be like. If it is, he didn't want to go there, to be bored for ever and ever.

Then miraculously they were at the end of the song. The pastor began to pronounce the benediction. Another thirty seconds and he could wriggle out of the pew and escape into the fresh air where he could spend a few minutes roaring round with his friends. Church was over for another week.

THE PROBLEM WITH CHILDREN IN THE CHURCH

For many children whose parents are regular church goers, the Sunday worship service is a refined form of torture. The facial expressions, and the body language speak eloquently about their feelings. Many churches recognize the problem and they don't want to instil such negative attitudes in their children. They have a brief family time of greeting and a prayer of blessing, and then send the children to a separate program in another hall.

The children generally prefer this option, but it reinforces in their minds the idea that church is incurably boring and no child should be expected to worship.

There is also a rising movement among parents that they would like to have their children worshipping with them on Sundays. Personally I wish this could happen because children need to see their parents showing their love to God.

However, before that can happen the church has to accept that the children have a significant place in the congregation. The children need to understand what is happening, to sense the awe of God's presence and to enter into the joy of praising Him. This doesn't happen by accident. Someone needs to train them in the processes of worship so they can sense God's presence for themselves.

Chapter 11. Worship and Celebration

Jesus encouraged the children to worship. He didn't object to their noise or enthusiasm.

> "When the chief priests and the teachers of the law saw the wonderful things He did and the children shouting in the temple, "Hosanna to the Son of David," they were indignant.
>
> "Do you hear what these children are saying?" they asked Him.
>
> "Yes," replied Jesus. "Have you never read, "from the lips of children and infants, You have ordained praise.""

In a celebrative atmosphere the children discover that being in God's presence is fun. At the same time, they should feel goose-bumps when know they are meeting the Lord of the Universe. We constantly reminded the children of how much God enjoys their worship. It is like preparing a surprise party for him and standing on tiptoe while He opens the door.

We also need to find ways for children to receive Bible teaching at their own level of understanding. This is the one place in Children's Ministry when a age-graded method of teaching is useful. Pre-schoolers have a very short concentration span and they learn best when there is plenty of movement, and repetition and story and music. Junior primary ages are beginning to learn the wonder of facts and questions and problems and answers. They do not learn easily in a logical word-based presentation of the message. The ability to think through a reasoned proposition does not begin till their early teens.

For this reason, the Faith Community Baptist Church decided to have Age Graded Children's celebrations for most Sundays. We decided to group them in broad age-bands – Nursery/Pre-School; Junior Primary and Intermediate. At this time of rapid growth in the church, there were many children in each age-band and there were trained leaders at each level. However within the age-bands, the children were not divided into sub-groups

NURSERY/PRE-SCHOOL

The ages of the children in this celebration were a bit flexible. They had to feel comfortable in the presence of other children and they had to be willing to take instructions and participate. Most children grew to become models and leaders to the younger children, but there came a time when they were ready to join the older children at Primary Level.

The aim of this Group was to introduce the children to the idea of worshipping God through movement and imagination. They would also learn about God and begin to follow of Jesus. It was amazing how much these little ones did learn over the period. They could remember the messages well and learned how to apply them. They learned through action, role-plays and drama to re-inforce the truth. Rhyming couplets were easy to learn and hard to forget.

Most of them understood God in terms of their imaginations, so it was important to portray him as close, loving, accessible and interested in everything about their lives; which of course, He is.

They loved to worship him with instruments, movements, banners, pictures and praise shouts. They learned to pray aloud, very briefly and very directly.

The stories emphasized the feelings of the characters. "How did the poor lady feel, who lost her money? Let's feel sorry for her. How did she feel when she found it? Let's be happy for her." "How would you feel if you lost your pet? How would you feel when you found it again? God feels just like that.!'

The other aim of the celebration is to prepare the children for joining in the intergenerational Celebration with the whole church. Parents were encouraged to see how the children worship and to encourage them to sing and pray with the adults. They liked standing on the seats with Mum or Dad's arm around them and worshipping with the big people.

JUNIOR PRIMARY CELEBRATION

Once the children entered Primary School Celebration they were very keen to come. It was not modelled on a school but rather on an adult worship celebration but scaled down to the children's level of understanding. When they entered to intergenerational Celebration they could see that it was just like their celebration on a different level.

The worship songs are active and lively but they are worshipful. There are many children's songs which are fun and noisy, but they are not intended to be worship songs. The aim of the worship is to draw the children into God's presence, to find out what He is like and to help them enjoy to enjoy his love and friendship. There is so much they can thank Him for. Every new discovery a child makes about the world he lives in, is a revelation of the God who made it. Everything they learn about Jesus is a cause for praise.

The celebration would open with faster active praise songs and after a time would move into more reflective songs of love for Jesus. Most of the songs had a choreography when their children could use their bodies to express the meaning. For celebration songs we combined dance and marching and in the slower songs we learn to do basic sign language[60] in a synchronised form. Movement is as important as the music because the children need to feel the song in their bodies as well as in their heads. The children focussed their minds on the words so that they could create the appropriate signs. Sometimes we would create our own signs to interpret the song.

In this stage we explained what the songs mean and why we are signing them. We told them how God is so happy when He hears them sing and sees them use their bodies to praise Him. We interspersed the songs with prayer and words of praise.. Often we encouraged the children to make up their own songs and sometimes they would bring their own instruments to add to the praise.

At times of reflection we would sometimes pause to allow the children to close their eyes, hear the music and sign the actions without actually singing the words. In the peace of the moment we would ask God to speak into the minds of the children to give them words or pictures. Sometimes the children expressed some profound ideas even when they didn't have the words to explain them.

---

60. Sign language is a language performed by our hands. It is used by the deaf as a way to communicate.

Chapter 11. Worship and Celebration

One girl of nine told us that she had seen a perfect flower that was so very beautiful, but as she watched a petal fell off. She heard God say that she was a beautiful as a flower, but when she disobeyed him, it was if a petal fell off her flower.

Another small boy was very excited about a monster he had seen. The leaders were a bit sceptical but they asked him to tell them more. He said that the monster was alike all the bad things in the world, but he was going out to fight the monster.

Don't you feel afraid of such a terrible monster?" the leader asked. "No," he said, "I've got Jesus on my side."

THE BIBLE MESSAGE

Junior Primary is a very demanding and productive period of the child's spiritual journey. Many of the children will make a first commitment to following Jesus and this will lead into the first stages of discipleship. It is a time of questions and clarification. They need to know the facts and to know that they are facts. Far too many children have a good knowledge of Bible stories but they are not aware that the events are historically true. When we begin a story with "Once upon a time…" or "Long, Long ago…" they get the message that this is a story like a fairy story. It didn't really happen. Picture books and visual aids sometimes re-inforce this message. Did Noah really sail the flood with a giraffe's head sticking out from one end and an elephant from the other? When we tell a parable we should begin like this. "This is a story which Jesus told when he was living here on the earth. Many children who could win a Bible quiz would not know whether the events "really happened."

It is important that the children do not pick up mistakes in their understanding, which will hold them back for years to come. They get impressions from the way we teach the Bible which certainly would not want them to believe. For instance, many children think Jesus is nice and God is angry. This is totally untrue since God's character is displayed in the character of Jesus. Yet that uneasiness about God can be carried into adult life.

The presentations had many styles of communication. Often there was drama, or real-life role plays. If the Pastor chose a difficult topic or something that would run on for some weeks, we devised a serial story which could make the same point and would maintain the interest over several weeks. We would always clarify which parts of the story were fact and which parts were illustration.

Sometimes we would invite a visitor to tell us a testimony story which illustrated the Bible theme. The children liked to be able to talk to the adult and ask question about their experience.

In the latter part of the service the children separated into small groups where they could talk about what they heard and they could ask questions. We would ask each other what we should do about the message. Was there something we should promise, or plan to do. Were there things to remember, or things we should stop doing? Was there something we could do to help other people? This application time was very open and usually this was reported to the intergenerational cell groups during the week.

THE INTERMEDIATES – THE BARNABAS CLUB

For the 11 – 13 year olds, the celebration took the form of an Equipping Club. They still had worship and a message but the purpose behind the presentation was that the children should be able to actively lead the group and also enter into ministry in other areas of life. The children were encouraged to pray about their own ministry gifts and to find out how the Holy Spirit was speaking to them.

Some children felt the worship was the major ministry that was calling their hearts. Many of these were already learning music to a high level and they were exploring how they could use this talent to worship the Lord. Others learned how to dance in worship or use ribbons or banners. Some began to practise being worship leaders in groups or congregations. The adult worshippers would sometimes visit them to teach them or discover what they were doing.

Some children felt called to prayer, both worship prayer and intercession. If there was a special event, they would pray to support it. Often they prayed in the groups for other children who had needs. In the intergenerational groups or the adult services, they would pray for adults who invited them to do so. They also learned to pray outside the church. A couple of groups walked their schools, silently praying for all the people who were involved. If a cell group had a prayer walk, the children would join in.

Still other children wanted to be able to tell their friends about Jesus. They practised using the children's guidebook which as pictorial and easy to explain to other children. Some of them learned how to present a short talk to other children or in the cell group.

In the children's celebration, children had the opportunity to get to know the Holy Spirit's gifts. They would listen to hear any word God might put in their minds and often He did. Their simple words would become prophetic.

One year we had a weekend camp for the Barnabas children. They would choose between four workshops, "Worship", "Prayer" "Message" and "Reaching Out to Others." Their parents came to visit the camp on the Saturday evening so they could see what the children had prepared. It was amazing. Six weeks later the church held a special Children's service to which all the children could invite their friends and families. It was packed with people, all except for the Prayer Group, who were praying in a separate room. The Worship children led the worship. One 12tewlve-year-old girl gave the message and invited people to get to know Jesus for themselves. When an invitation was given many children asked to follow Jesus and they were counselled by the Barnabas children.

CELEBRATION WITH THE ADULTS

When a church separates the children from the adult congregation, it is not an ideal solution. Often there are practical difficulties which constrict our opportunities for the mean time. One of them may be the numbers of people who meet in the worship space. It is hard to keep families together. Sometimes the adults are not ready to receive the children. They feel the children have invaded their worship and they cannot feel at peace.

The adults need to be trained as much as the children. They have been accustomed to feeling comfortably isolated from their normal world during their worship. It's safe and protected but they have never yet experienced the amazing joy of being the family of God together. Until they have discovered the joy and blessing of having the children with them, nothing will change. The pastors and leaders need to preach and to practise intergenerational worship. We needed to start with some pilot services to show the adults how it might work. There were some mistakes, but we all have to learn how to help each other be in God's presence together.

For this reason, the leaders of the Faith Community Church developed a plan to introduce the children into the adult service by stages. It was a revelation to many people. It also took a lot of effort from very committed people.

On the last Sunday of the month, our services became intergenerational. That means that the children came to the adults' services with their parents and stayed all the way through. It was not a Children's Service which the adults had to tolerate. It was a spiritual experience in which everyone participated. Most of the families brought all their children to the service. There was an audio-crèche for some mothers who wanted to care for their infants while they listened to the worship. In some families some older children partnered with younger ones to help them keep focussed on what was happening. Some families included grandparents or single aunts and uncles as part of the family experience.

1. Worship and Prayer
The key to bringing the whole church into worship, was the willing co-operation of the Music team with the Children's Ministry. We discussed and planned which was appropriate

to the theme but was accessible to the children. It did not have to be "children's" music but we did need to rehearse it first in the Children's Celebration and explain to the children how the songs were helping us to come near to God. Even if they couldn't read every word, they did catch the mood and message of the songs. Some of the parents allowed their children to take off their shoes and stand on the seats so they could link hands and sing together.

On the stage we had two experienced children's leaders who joined the worship team and modelled for the children what they were supposed to be doing. This included action and movement. During the celebration some children produced percussion instruments. Some of them danced with ribbons in the aisles. As the music became more reflective, those things were put away and we moved into gentler, smoother actions.

When the church moved into prayer with a prayer leader in front, the words of his/her prayer were displayed on the visual screen, so that the children could keep up with the words. Sometimes the church was invited to pray for things in families and to include non-family people. In another intergenerational church, I saw the Pastor ask if anyone in the church wanted the children to pray for them. They had trained older children to form teams of three to go out into the congregation to pray for anyone who raised their hands. It was a powerful demonstration of the effectiveness of children in prayer.

2. The Bible Message
The Bible message was probably the hardest part of the service to present to such a varied congregation. It didn't just happen. We had to plan ahead and work hard to incorporate the children. We started by issuing every primary age and intermediate age child with a nice hard-back notebook.

Chapter 11. Worship and Celebration

Younger children could have a notebook if they wanted it but if not, they received a visual based on the theme of the message.

When the Pastor began to preach, the children would open the notebook and write down the title and the Bible passage of the message. We had an experienced children's leader working in the visual screen department to help the children follow what the Pastor was saying and to write some of it down.

As our Pastor preached, our children's ministry leader wrote notes in simple sentences on to the screen. Sometimes there would be a question to answer. Sometimes a simple sketch. Key words were highlighted. The children were copying into their notebooks from the visual screen. They were also encouraged to write down any of their own thoughts or questions if they wished to do so. Later they would share their notebooks with their parents or their cell groups. Once a quarter they could show their notebooks to the children's leaders and get awards for their efforts. It was always moving to see what they had recorded.

When it came time for the invitation, sometimes children would go to the front for prayer. Children's leaders were available but they also had senior children to help pray for these children. Parents could also join them if they wished.

It was not easy to provide intergenerational worship in a church where there were over a thousand children in the ministry. Sometimes families went to different services on the Sunday. Occasionally the whole church met in a sports stadium so we could show the unity of the Body of Christ. Even on the large scale, Intergenerational Worship and Celebration could work. It needed everybody to co-operate with everybody so that everybody could be included.

In a smaller church the project is more informal and practical. When most people know each other's families, there are more possibilities of including the children. Many parents wish rather wistfully that they could have their children in church, but assume it isn't possible. It can be done, if only we are prepared to work hard to welcome all the ages, and teach them how to worship and hear the word of the Lord.

It is a very good idea for parents, cell leaders and some other adults to visit the Children's Sunday Celebration at every level. It will help the adults realise what the children are capable of doing and how it can enrich their cell group. Many adults have no idea that children can hear the Word of the Lord for themselves, or can pray for someone else. It widens their vision of how they can incorporate the children into their group.

3. Memory Verse
Many people think of memory verses as an investment for the future. It will be so good to remember them in our old age, and so it will. But for the children the best benefits are here and now. The memory verse is a resource for using all kind of ministry and spiritual gifts.

When a child is learning to pray aloud, they can turn a memory verse into a prayer.

Psalm 56:3 "When I am afraid, I put my trust in you," could become, "Dear Lord Jesus, help me not to be afraid because I know I can put our trust in you. Amen"

Or if praying for another person it might sound like this, "Lord Jesus, I want to pray for my friend Michelle, that she will not be afraid of the bullies at school. Let her trust in You." Amen

Or if a child is giving a word of encouragement he might pray, "The Lord says that when you are afraid when you go to Japan, you can trust in Him because he will be with you." Or it might even be a word of prophecy. "Lord, we know some bad things are happening in the world but we will not be afraid because we know we can trust in you."

When the children use Bible verses to speak to others, they know they are saying words of truth.

In an intergenerational cell the children should be encouraged to use their memory verses and teach them to the other cell members. A leader might ask a child if they have a memory verse to share with the group especially if it is relevant to the theme.

For children their memory verses are like tools or weapons to cope with life. When they run into problems or awkward situations, the Holy Spirit can use a memory verse to calm the child's spirit and to help them know what to do.

4. Helping Children to Worship in the Cell Group

Children do not usually learn to worship in the cell group, but rather in their families or in the Sunday Celebration. When they join the cell group they do not automatically start to worship. They need to be encouraged to join in especially when there are songs they know. The more they participate in the worship, they more they want to be involved. One three-year old thought it was his duty to give out the song sheets to everyone.

It is a good idea for the cell leader and some other adults to visit the Children's Celebration at some time. When they see what the children can do they will have confidence to give them good opportunities in the cell group. Sometimes the children might plan to lead the whole worship in the cell group. Some children have gifts of music they can share with everyone.

TO THINK ABOUT

1. Can you remember being in a worship service as a child? Did it touch your heart? Did you feel God close to you?

2. What could you do to help your children worship in a Sunday Service?

3. How could you help the adults receive and accept the children sharing in a worship service?

4. Have you ever heard a child pray aloud, or prophecy, or give a word of blessing?

Chapter 12

GETTING TO KNOW CHILDREN AND MAKING THEM YOUR FRIENDS

An elderly gentleman in a church some years ago, felt friendly towards the children and wanted to get to know them. But he was rather unbending in his style and didn't know how to greet them. It was his habit to pat them on the head or even chuck them under the chin and say gruffly, "My, my, what a big boy/girl you're getting to be."

One girl of eleven really disliked this familiarity. One day when he was sitting down, she approached the gentleman, chucked him under the chin, and said, "You're getting to be a really old gentleman, aren't you?"

His heart was in the right place, but he didn't know that when you want to make friends with children, you must show them respect. Children do not like to be talked down to, and you mustn't assume too much on a first acquaintance. Young children do not like to be hugged or kissed by a stranger. Older children do not like to be reminded of their size. All children like to be given some space to find out who you are and how they are going to relate to you.

STEPS IN MAKING FRIENDS WITH A CHILD

1. Conversation Openers
When you first meet someone, you talk about neutral things that you both know about. With adults it could be the weather, your job, current events or sports. Older adults like to talk about their state of health or the minor frustrations of the world. With a children's limited experience, you need to start with something they do. Sometimes you can start a conversation by praising them for something they have done. Ask them to tell you more about what happened. Or you might talk about school or holidays, or their family, or television or even computer games.

2. Finding Common Ground
As you begin the conversation, you are looking for the light to go on. You can be talking on a level of mere politeness and suddenly you notice that something has really caught their attention. With children it is hard to pick what that will be. It could be garden bugs, or dinosaurs or small animals, princesses or wolves. Sometimes their tee-shirts will give you a clue. If you ever get to visit their home, you will find it in the things they use to decorate their bedrooms. You can't be expected to know much about their chosen interest, but you have a great capacity to learn, and they may have a great capacity to tell you about it.

After that, you notice when those interests appear in the world around you. Next time you see the child you tell them what you discovered and renew the conversation. When they think you are interested, they will return to you with more news.

In one group of boys, the leader could not get to know one boy very well. He was quiet and cooperative but he also shy and silent. He didn't seem to be interested in the things most of the boys were excited about. At last the leader asked his parents what were the boy's hobbies and they told him that his passion in life was breeding canaries.

The leader knew absolutely nothing about canaries but he took the first chance to visit the local public library and find some books on canaries. As soon as he had learned some basics, he went to the boy's home and asked, "Would you show me your canaries?" The boy didn't need a second invitation. Out in the aviary they discussed all manner of things, how canaries mated, how long it takes the eggs to hatch, how to produce colour differences. The leader learned more about canaries than he planned for. But he also made a friend. From that time the boy was excited about his leader. They always had something to talk about, and they could also talk about the important things of life in general. It is a great investment to get to know a child.

3. Sharing Life Stories

As a friendship develops, most people want to know more about their new friend. What is their family like; what is their life history; what special events have happened? This is harder for children because their life experience is so much shorter, and they can't even remember some parts of it. Sometimes they only half understand important events that have happened. Imagination and memory can get mixed up in a version which they tell you. Just keep an open mind until you can understand a little better.

However, they love to hear your life story. In the olden days before they were born, amazing things happened and they want to know what life was like then. They will want to know about your wife and family and where you live and whether you have pets. They want to know about your sports and your hobbies and the work you do and where you go for your holidays. Your life is a whole new window into someone else's reality and they add your experience to their knowledge of the world.

We always encourage cell members especially Kids' Slot members to be open in sharing their life story. You don't have to pretend to be perfect. They won't believe you anyway. But if you can tell about some of your mistakes and what you did to fix them, they will add that to their databanks. Most of all the children will want to know how you decided to follow Jesus and what difference that has made to your life. There is nothing stronger that first-hand experience.

Children will tell you many things about themselves and their world. Not all of them will be true or they may be exaggerated. Often they may not have understood the events which they witnessed around them. Sometimes the facts may be all too true and someone is telling them not to talk about it. Be careful and prayerful with such information. Sometimes the child may need a sympathetic explanation from someone they trust. Sometimes a wise and helpful person may need to get to know the family to discover if the child is safe. This is a family matter and we have a responsibility which should be shared with your Pastor.

4. Share Your Hopes and Dreams

When our son was about six years old, the height of his ambition was to drive the trolley which carried the luggage from the air terminal to the plane. It fascinated him. We hoped that he would one day go to college and have a professional career. At six years old he didn't care about college. So we would take time to drive to the airport and let him watch the man drive the luggage trolleys across the tarmac.

If you are very fortunate, children will tell you some of their dream and hopes for the future. Everything seems possible to them at this stage of life. So we need to treat their dreams with great tenderness. We can explore the possibilities and do some dreaming with them. One day the dream will change and we need to be ready to let that happen.

If the friendship is really mutual you would also share some of your dreams with your child-friend. Children are amazingly understanding when you tell them of your hopes and fears. They will get excited for you. They will pray for you. They will show enthusiasm when you take tests or interviews. My childhood leader had a vision of going to the mission field. We prayed for her right through Bible College, right through missionary training. We all wanted to be her bridesmaids. And we all learned about God's call to missionary service. She was an example and a model.

5. Warning!
If children trust you enough to tell you some of their inner life, never repeat it to others, or make a joke about it. Sometimes they will say things which are unconsciously funny. We may long to share the joke with someone, even their parents. But this is not fair to the child. If they find out you have broken their confidence, they will find it hard to trust you again.

The cell group should be a safe place for children. The adults must make sure that the children are protected while they are in the group. Sometimes the men in the group like to have a partner to help them lead Kids' Slot. The level of rumour and suspicion in our society has become so high, that they are afraid to get close to children at all and certainly not alone. This is tragic because the children need safe adult friends and role models among men. If a person is known to have a weakness or history of inappropriate behaviour towards children, they should never be left alone with them in the cell group. Cell members should protect each other.

6. Sharing the Lives of Children.
Children can be inconvenient friends at times. They will often ignore you at first, but once they learn that they are allowed to talk to you, they can come bouncing into your life regardless of what you are doing. It's better to plan out times when you can touch base with them. It doesn't always have to be long times.

A short visit to a sport's match, where you can cheer them on for a while, makes you keen supporter. One cell leader took the time to see a child perform in a school concert. The child was amazed that he would come, even when he didn't have to.

When I was sick in bed at seven years old, an old lady from church came by to give me an orange and a book to read. She didn't want it returned. I loved the story and I still have her book on my bookshelves. She was my friend. Friendships which you build with a child can last for a life-time.

7. Keeping the Attention of the Group
It is important in a group that every child in the group is recognised by name and by a moment's personal attention. As you begin to talk to individuals, draw other children into the conversation so that the group develops a body life together. Sometimes you might sit an older child next to a younger one or a new child so they can help each other.

Your eyes are your best tools for gaining the attention of the children. As you let your eyes wander around the group, you catch the eye of each child so they know you are aware of them. Your watchful eyes should not be always reproving. Your eyes can laugh, commend and encourage the children so they can feel your approval. A look of sadness or disappointment is quickly transmitted. Even an insensitive child feels uncomfortable when he is confronted with a questioning stare.

Your eyes will also help you bring more children into the conversation. A look or smile will encourage a shy child to speak up. If the child is trying to do well, your eyes can show your genuine approval.

8. The Floor is a Great Leveller

Children often feel at a disadvantage because of their height difference with adults. Mabel was an older widow, whose children had grown up and her grandchildren lived far away. She enjoyed talking with the children in church on Sunday. As she greeted a child, she would sit down or drop to one knee so she could talk to the child, eyeball to eyeball. Whenever she talked to one child, other children would come running up to get into the conversation too. They liked the lady who was willing to come to their height.

For children the world is too big. People can be several feet taller than they are. Chairs and tables are the wrong size. Food is served above their heads. When you get down to the same level as the children you are showing respect for them. Of course child-size chairs and table are not easy for adults to use either.

The floor is a great leveller. Adults and children who sit on the floor are on equal terms. They can see each other's faces and respond directly to one another. Eye contact is easy and everyone is included.

If a young child gets restless, they can move around without disturbing the group. We had a hyperactive boy in our group. He would leave the circle and turn a forward roll. He would lie on his stomach or his back. The group took no notice. He would come back into the group when he was ready, and he was never out of control.

When adults and children sit on chairs, any movement is noisy. Children can think of dozens of different things to do with a chair and all of them are noisy. No leader wants to try to control children and furniture at the same time.

9. The Power of Praise

When children come to a cell group, they should not expect to be scolded all the time. Sometimes parents are so anxious about their children, they are on edge waiting for something bad to happen. If there is an atmosphere of disapproval, the children will be afraid to open up and talk to the adults. Parents, leaders and all the adults need to be ready for good things to happen. As soon as a child does something worthy of praise, someone should speak words of appreciation and approval. The child may be surprised at the good feeling they get when they have done something well. They may be even more surprised to discover the God is pleased with them too.

Children also need to be encouraged to affirm each other. Sibling rivalry can cause friction in families. In many societies children suffer severe peer pressure from their friends. Children can laugh at each other's mistakes, and overlook their achievements. "Being good," can be seen as being anti-social. Trading insults may be part of the chatter of the "cool" kids.

Children need to learn to appreciate each other, even the young ones. They may enjoy a friend's success without envy, and encourage a child who has failed. There are not many environments in life where a child can learn to give and receive appreciation.

10. The Power of Prayer

Prayer is an effective tool for controlling children's behaviour. Prayer before the meeting can certainly help the atmosphere. But it is also very powerful during the meeting. Restless and chatter may arise from boredom or cramped conditions. The Enemy can supply plenty of distractions to break up the group.

In a negative atmosphere, prayer is a spiritual weapon to bring the power and peace into the situation. Sometimes we need to stop what we are doing and ask for the Holy Spirit to touch our hearts to bring his peace and order. We may even pray for an individual child in a positive way. "Dear Father, we know that Jason is such a great kid and he has a very busy mind, and you know that too. Please come close to him so he can feel your presence and start to praise You. Amen.

One day in our Children's Church, we had a visiting group of puppeteers. They hadn't prepared well enough and things were going very wrong. The children were not slow to notice that the puppets' mouths were not moving at the right times and there was a lot of backstage giggling. The story-line was lost. The children began to laugh and wriggle and get out of control. The puppet team left hastily and left us with three hundred riotous children. It seems nothing could calm them down.

Our Children's Pastor was a quiet lady. On this Sunday she just walked to the microphone and began to pray. In the name of Jesus she banished any spirit of disobedience and rebellion from the room. She claimed the space for Jesus and asked the Holy Spirit to enter every child's heart with peace and praise. At the same time the musicians began to play quiet music and in less than a minute all the children were praising God.

We should never forget that atmosphere and space and personal relations are spiritual dimensions.

11. Encouraging Children to Talk

When people are new to doing Kids' Slot, they often ask how they can make the children keep quiet. They remember their own childhood when children were expected to be quiet in the presence of adults. I usually explain to them that a cell group is not a place where the leader talks while the children are silent. It is a place for shared conversation, where the leader guides the discussion. For some adults this feels quite threatening. They fear that if the children start talking, they will interrupt the discussion and miss the point.

In fact, interruption is a great learning moment. They want to know something and we can divert it back to the point. It is a skill we can learn. We should never ignore an irrelevant comment especially from a younger child. We may silence them, but we have lost their attention.

A child may interrupt your flow with a thought in his/her own mind. "I got new shoes. See?" The leader does not choke, or brush the words away. He/she acknowledges what the child said and tries to lead the idea back to the point.

"So you have. Aren't they beautiful? Did Mummy buy those for you? I bet Zacchaeus wished that he had a Mummy to buy him nice new shoes. He didn't have anyone who loved him. No one wanted to be his friend. He was very lonely. He wondered if Jesus might be his friend…"

When you allow the children to speak it shows that you want to hear what they are thinking. Some children will have heard the Bible stories many times before. They will be glad to help you tell the story or to add some feelings. You can ask them what the story means or whether they know of anyone else who may have been in the same situation.

Often with older children you will discover that they have acquired some false understandings of the story. They can repeat back the basic facts but they can miss the point. When I talk to children about the wise man and the foolish man, I often ask them was the story is supposed to tell us. Most children think it is about house-building. If you are going to build a house it needs good foundations underneath it. I have some nine-year-old children who think there might be something spiritual about it but they are not sure what. Nine-year-olds are not very good as seeing abstract meaning behind the practical facts.

12. The Hidden Message

Children know when the adults are glad to see them go. They can tell which adults don't want to talk to them. If none of the men in the cell group want to lead the Kids' Slot they learn that men don't want to be bothered with children. Worse still they may learn that Christian faith is for women, and real men keep their distance. They know what it means when the leader is constantly looking at his watch.

When we deal with children our hearts must be open and genuine. We must laugh at our own mistakes and tell the children how we are feeling. We can seek their prayer and help and they will respect us even more. If we want to feel comfortable with the children, we need to talk with them or play with them during the fellowship time. They begin to own you as a friend.

If you need to talk to a child personally, do it in a public place where there are other people around. Listen more than you talk. Sometimes children just want to talk about something but they are not asking you to fix it. They just want to tell you how they feel. If they want to know what you think, they will ask you.

Do not condemn what they say even if the problem seems trivial. No one wants to feel stupid when they've asked a question. Don't assume they are wrong. Children are good observers, even if they cannot understand how the world works. If they find it hard to explain what they are asking, let them draw pictures as they talk. They can give you clues better than words. Sometimes you need to make an agreement to find out more about the question before next week's meeting.

An adult friend can be a great assent to a family. If the child is worrying about a an internal friction or quarrel, they sometimes need someone who is trusted and objective. Parents should value such a friend to help smooth things out.

Amanda, a thirteen-year-old, was furious with her parents because they didn't want her to wear lipstick. The girl flounced out of the house in a rage and found her adult "aunty." "You'll never believe how mean my parents are being to me. They won't let me wear lipstick like the other girls. They think I'm just a baby." Aunty opened the cookie jar and offered a drink. As they talked she let Amanda vent her feelings. At last Aunty looked at Amanda reflectively and observed, "When you do start to wear make-up, you'll need to get some very good tuition, because doing it on your own can be a risk. Actually I hope you'll leave it for a bit longer, because just at this moment your skin is the best it will ever look in your whole life, and I wouldn't want to mess it up."

"So you agree with them," frowned Amanda.

"Well, I've always thought that you start to apply make-up when you start to develop skin problems and you are losing that amazing freshness. You know, when pimples start to pop up and your eyes start looking tired. By that time, you might need some colour to highlight your face to make it more attractive. But at the moment I think you look stunning. I've seen girls a lot older than you who don't look nearly as good. Why don't we both have a talk with your parents and make a plan about when you should start make-up and how you should learn to do it really well, so you look wonderful and not just self-taught."

Amanda was looking thoughtful. "I think I know what you mean. Some of my friends do overdo it a bit. I'd really like you to come with to talk to my parents. I don't want to make them angry but I don't like being treated like a child."

Amanda's parents should be grateful for their wise friend. Another hurdle had been cleared.

TO THINK ABOUT

1. When you were growing up, did you have an adult friend you could talk to when you wanted someone else's opinion?

2. Do you know a child outside your family who is your friend now? What do you like to talk about?

3. Practise a conversation in which you meet a child for the first time and try to make friends.

Part Three

THE SPIRITUAL GROWTH OF CHILDREN.
A CHILD'S FAITH – A PERSONAL TESTIMONY

When I was nine-years old I felt God was asking me to be baptised. I had witnessed several baptismal services and I listened very carefully to what the preacher said. He made it very clear that once a person decides to follow Jesus, the next step of obedience is to be baptised.

I knew I had made that decision but I was a bit afraid of baptism. I wanted to obey Jesus but I was also afraid of being submerged in water. In spite of my fear, I asked my parents if I could be baptised, but they were very doubtful. They knew the elders of the church did not approve of baptising children.

Reluctantly my father spoke to the leading elder, who suggested that, if I was really serious, I should arrange to meet the elders myself. He felt sure that would be too much of a barrier.

However, the next Sunday I went up to the leading elder and asked if I could talk to the elders about being baptised. He kindly gathered them together and they spent some time gently telling me that I was too young and I should come back when I was older. I kept telling them that Jesus never turned any children away, and in the end they relented and agreed that I should be baptised, and should share in the Lord's Supper.

Some people wondered if it was wise to let a child take such a step. Could I really understand what it was all about? Probably not as much as I do now, but I did know that I was doing what Jesus wanted me to do and it was a very special moment for me when I was immersed and rose out of the pools in great thankfulness.

Remembering Jesus at the Lord's Supper became the highlight of my week. I learned to enter into worship and love Him more and more. At one time there was a poliomyelitis epidemic in New Zealand and all the children were forbidden to go to school or church for three months. How I missed the Lord's Supper! Then I began to celebrate the Lord's Supper at home using orange juice and bread. Since I was an only child, there were just the two of us, Jesus and me.

Chapter 13

SPIRITUAL AWARENESS STARTS IN THE FAMILY

To a new-born baby the world is a mystery. They do not know the reasons for anything. They need to function in the world long before they can understand how it works. They learn to press buttons and the television shows a picture. But they still think there is a little man in there talking to them.

It is hard for us to conceive how little a new-born baby knows. When Mom and Dad bring their new son home, he is surrounded with bunny rabbit toys and cuddle rugs and diapers, but he is not aware of them. He is not even aware that there are two people called, "Mommy" or "Daddy". He only feels the warm touch of a gentle body as his hunger is satisfied.

Many years ago I was talking to a Christian man who had recently become a father. He told me quite casually that the previous night he had spanked his new baby. I was shocked.

"Why did you do such a thing?" I gasped.

He said that the baby had woken up his parents five times during the night, so he decided to teach the child that the behaviour was not allowed. He wanted to set up good discipline in the family. He didn't know he was abusing his child.

He thought the baby could think like an older child or adult. He couldn't imagine the limited world in which the baby lived. Baby didn't know that Mommy and Daddy were trying to sleep. He couldn't count the number of times he had cried out. He didn't even know that there were two adult people in the room who had a separate existence from his own. All he knew was that he was cold, or wet, or in pain, or hungry or lonely.

Often adults transfer their own thinking into the minds of their children. They expect the children to know far more than they really do. That's why children so often looked shocked when they are scolded for something. They cannot associate the anger with their actions. Not being able to understand what is going on in a young child's mind is one of the most frustrating experiences of parenthood.

THINKING OUR WAY BACK TO CHILDHOOD

Children are not born with the ability to think logically. That doesn't develop until they are in upper elementary school. As little children they collect data from the world they experience and try to fit it into patterns which are not based on facts.

Their great tool of thought is imagination. They can explore unlimited possibilities, without any boundaries of mere facts. They create random worlds, which make perfect sense to them on the limited experience they have. They don't need reasons or explanations. It's just the way things are.

Pre-schoolers will believe what you tell them. They accept the story at face value, even if they do not fully understand it. If you tell them that Jonah was swallowed by a great fish, they will believe you. They will also believe you if you tell them that Jonah swallowed the great fish. They haven't started to ask, "How does that happen?"

In their own inner thinking they accept all the possibilities their imagination can think up. The power of these early imaginary pictures lingers on as an adult impression.

I have a very early memory of a picture I had as a child. There was a gate in a fence near my house. I remember imagining myself going through that gate and finding something awful on the other side. I don't know what it was, but to this day, if I see a gate similar to that one, I feel a sense of unease. On the positive side, children can imagine some wonderful pictures and experiences which light up the ordinary world in which they live.

FINDING GOD IN THE IMAGINATION

1. Someone is in Charge

God gave small children the gift of imagination so that they would have a channel to find him and communicate with Him. In fact, it is a surer way to find Him than our faulty intellect.

All children seem to have an innate belief that someone is in charge of the world. Even children who have never heard the word, "God", think that someone is making things happen. They see the changing of the weather. They see plants growing and insects crawling. They see people and animals dying and giving birth. They experience night and day, tides going in and out, storms and sunsets and they make up their own explanations of what is happening.

Even parents who actively discourage their children from believing in God, find at first, it is hard to convince their children that there is no one there. One child was told by her mother that there is no God, that he was only a fairy story. The child, when an adult, reported, "I never spoke about my own ideas to her, out of a sense of shame, feeling that I knew who God who and how God was, and she did not yet have that understanding.[61]

2. The World Ought To Be Fair

Children at a very young age seem to have an unshakeable belief that the world ought to be fair. Where they get this from is a mystery. Even children whose experience of life is one of abuse, neglect and unfairness, seem to feel that they have been cheated. Life is not supposed to be like that. My own red-headed daughter used to plant her feet firmly on the ground and declare, "It's not fair, Daddy. It's just not fair."

Often children take a step further and blame the unfairness on God. Sometimes they try to find excuses or explanations. They often struggle with serious problems of life, before they have the vocabulary to put it into words.

An excellent example of this is recorded by Edward Robinson in his book, "The Original Vision." A girl of five observed a "colony of ants running rapidly and purposefully about their business. All at once I knew that to them, I was invisible. I was

---

61. Robinson Edward, The Original Vision: A Study of the Religious Experience of Childhood. (New York: Seabury Press. 1983.) 62

able at one glance, to comprehend to some extent, the whole colony. I had the power to destroy or scatter it."[62]

The girl than looked up at the sky and felt how small she was by comparison.

And yet she was part of it all. She suddenly realised that if an enormously large person was watching her, he would be to her, the same as she was to the ants, beyond understanding, but she would be part of him. She was so pleased with this idea that she ran in to her mother and announced, "Mommy, we're just like ants running around on a giant's tummy."

It must have seemed very bizarre to her mother, but to the little girl it made perfect sense. She had made a profound discovery about the inability of creatures of one kind to communicate with creatures of another kind – the eternal gap between God, who is Spirit, and we, who are mortal.

3. God, the Super-parent
The major model that children have for God, is their parents. Because parents are the major authority in their lives, it seems that the Person who is in charge of everything in the world must be like them, only bigger.

Clearly He ought to have more power and wisdom to be able to deal with everyone's problems, but His management style and His attitudes are usually influenced by the authority figures they know. If their parents are loving and understanding, the children imagine that God will be like that. If they are unpredictable and angry, then God will be frightening. If their parents are carping and judgmental, that's the way the

---

62. Ibid

children will imagine God. If they are distant and remote and show little interest in their children, then God will also seem uninterested and far off. These personal experiences in the home are far more powerful than any formal teaching they may receive in church. Their childhood impressions linger with them throughout life and may help or hinder their adult relationship with God.

In my conferences in churches around the world, I sometimes asked people if they liked God when they knew him in childhood. On average, about half the people would signify that they did not. Even children who had accepted Jesus as Saviour often reported a lurking fear of God, the Father. They did not like the idea that God was watching them all the time and waiting to catch them doing something bad.

It is hard for them to believe that God really likes them. They imagine that God is holding them up as if in a pair of tweezers, saying, "Look at this repulsive little human creature. However, because I am God, I will love him." This is a travesty on the nature of God. He is more like a Father who sees His child trying to walk, and exclaims, "Look at my child, I'm so pleased with him/her.

Most children do not believe that God is anywhere nearby. He's somewhere in outer space, keeping an eye on things but not close enough to get involved in our lives. When we say to children, "God is watching over you," that is not always a comfort. That's why they sometimes try to hide from God. As a child when I was doing something praiseworthy, I used to imagine that God was on the sidelines, cheering me on. If I was doing something mean or underhand, I hoped He wasn't looking my way.

Often when something bad happens to a child, the child feels that it happened because they were naughty and God is punishing them. This happens especially if a marriage breaks down. They feel it must be their fault. Of if Grandma dies, it must be because they made a loud noise and disturbed her.

As a child grows, this sense of being observed by God weakens and virtually disappears. But the echoes of distrust may linger for many years without any conscious explanation.

4. What is Right and Wrong?

Children make their own decisions about what is right or wrong from their own experiences and without too much logic. It does not depend solely on their teaching or lack of teaching. It comes from their sense of approval or disapproval. If they win approval from their parents or caregivers, they assume they have done something right. If they get scolded they learn that they have done something wrong.

Children do not allow for the fact that sometimes parents scold them because they are impatient, or worried, or frustrated. A father will yell at a child who interrupts his sport's program or who interrupts a telephone call. The moral value of the action is not under consideration. The scolding happens because the child has interfered with the desires of the parents.

Many children believe that parents do not sin. If no one scolds the parents, it means they do not do anything wrong. The parents set the rules so that makes them above the rules. It can be sadly disillusioning when the children reach the level when they recognise that their parents are very fallible people.

It is also very hard for children to evaluate the seriousness of their actions. They tend to judge the size of their sin but the amount of fuss that is made about it. A wrong deed which causes significant financial loss is more important than a sin of the spirit.

I have tried testing children to find out their perceptions on why an action is wrong. I ask a group of children to imagine a situation in which they are trying to help Mommy carry some cups in the cupboard. In the process the child accidentally drops one of Mom's best china cups, the one Dad bought her for her birthday. I ask the children what Mom would say.

They describe a great outcry with scolding and tears. It was such a special cup. They would have to pay for it out of their pocket money.

Then I asked the children, "Suppose Mommy had just put a fresh pitcher of juice into the refrigerator ready for her guests who were coming soon. She asked you not to touch it. You were feeling really thirsty and the juice looked good so you decided to take just a small drink before the guests came. You poured out a little juice into an old peanut paste tumbler, but as you did, your hand slipped and you dropped the tumbler breaking it. What would your mother say then?"

They all assured me that she would be mad at them, but not as mad as she was about the special birthday cup. She would yell at them and make them clean up the mess, but she wouldn't make them pay for the broken tumbler.

At this point I asked them which is the greater sin, breaking the special birthday cup or breaking the old tumbler. Up to the age of ten, they all agree that breaking the special birthday cup was the worst sin. I had some difficulty convincing them that the first example was not a sin, but just a clumsy accident. In the second case their intention had been to disobey, and it was a sin even if the cost had only been slight. The child needed to say sorry and ask forgiveness.

Many children misunderstand the nature of sin. Some people would say that it's foolish to use the word, "sin" when referring to the actions of children. But if they do not know how they have done wrong, they do not know why they are being blamed? They are bewildered when they are scolded and put it down to the irrationality of adults. They do not begin to learn the need for moral choice or why God wants them to live by His standards. Many children assume that if they are not scolded, then no wrong has been done and they have "got away with it." This attitude leads to serious behaviour problems in teenage years.

5. What Do Children Understand by Salvation?

In the family, children learn that if they do enough good things to please their parents, they will generally be regarded as a good and pleasing child. In their minds they contrast themselves with naughty children who are rude and disobedient and unacceptable. Often the "difficult" child has given up hope of winning their parents' attention by good behaviour so they try for some negative attention.

When the children transfer this idea into their relationship with God, there arises a misconception which seems to pervade the whole secular world. Most people who have a lingering idea of God, believe that if they do enough good things in their lifetime, they will make the grade and find their way into heaven. At the very least they should do more good things than bad things.

'I've always done my best," "I'm a decent sort of person, "I'm better than most people." It's like the pagan notion that our good deeds and our bad deeds will be weighed up, and if the scales tip slightly to the right, then we're 'in.' It's only fair.

This is the very opposite of the Gospel of Jesus Christ. God does not sit around measuring the colour of our actions. He offers free cleansing through the loving sacrifice which Jesus made for us on the cross. We can't get salvation by our own efforts or trying to be good.

So where does this idea come from. I don't know of any church that teaches that you can get to heaven by being good. People learn it in their families where their worth is measured on the basis of being good of bad. In that situation you cannot admit to being wrong. Wrong brings disapproval, anger, punishment. Many children find it hard to be truly sorry or to be truly forgiven. This misunderstanding can become part of a child's mindset, almost before we can identify it.

6. Forgiveness and Restoring Peace

If children are to learn to love and trust a God of love, they need to experience His love in the home. Anger and scolding is not forever. Genuine sorrow produces forgiveness and restoration of relationship. Many parents, having punished their children, forget the second half of the transaction – sweet words of acceptance and love. How quickly children respond to the hug or touch that says, "All if forgotten now. You are my dear child."

Friendship and laughter in the family is like an investment in family relationships. When you have some good times together, and the parents have demonstrated their unshakeable love for the child, it is possible to rebuke a child's behaviour without losing their trust.

One day my daughter had broken one of our family rules and she was scolded and gated for a week. She moaned loudly about the unfairness of it all, so much so that her teacher became aware of it. Calling my daughter after school, the teacher enquired if she could help with the bad relationship she had with her mother. My daughter looked at her in blank amazement.

"I don't have a bad relationship with my mother," she protested. "She's my best friend and she's a great mother. I just happen to be mad with her at the moment, but we still love each other."

Love is the life-breath of the home so the children think that God is like that too. Love is the life-breath of the universe.

7. Positive and Negative Words

It is very easy in the average busy household to get into bad habits of negative speech towards the children. We don't mean to nag them, but it comes out that way. I struggled with my youngest son at times when he was absentminded or disorganised. I had been goading him along trying to get to church on time. "Have you done this?" "Why haven't you done that?" "Are you still not ready?" At last we were all in the car, and I turned on the ignition. It gave a discouraging "Phut". "Oh (his name)" I scolded.

"What did I do?" he called from the back. Suddenly it hit me. I'd formed a habit of blaming the children for my frustrations when it wasn't their fault.

Every time we pour out our anger or frustration on a child, whether they deserve it or not, we are unconsciously pronouncing a curse on them. It becomes a self-fulfilling prophecy which they can't escape because their parents think they are no good.

On the other hand, when we praise our children and appreciate their effort they begin to believe they are acceptable. God helps them to live up to the image their parents have of them. They will try harder to win the positive words. They will do extra, and feel treasured. That's how God wants us all to feel about Him.

ADOPTING THE FAMILY WORLD VIEW

Young children often have strong opinions on all sorts of subjects. They know who should be voted into government, who are the people you can trust in society, what sports team to follow, what is the best make of car and what products to buy. Is this the result of careful rational thought? No. They have simply adopted the opinions and prejudices of their parents. These opinions are not lightly held. They are convinced they are right for the very good reason that "My Daddy says so!"

This kind of borrowed thinking is at the heart of most racial, social and gender prejudice. Even in adulthood value judgments are accepted without examination. It takes a major crisis to cause people to review their basic ideas and their way of life.

This also happens in religious faith. Some people accept the faith they were born into, without actually thinking it through themselves.

When we understand how many of the underlying ideas and attitudes of children originate in their homes during early childhood, we realise why God places so much importance on the family. The role modelling of the parents is far more important than formal teaching. If the parents are vibrant and consistent in their relationship with God, the children know that their faith is their cornerstone. Even in the midst of family disagreements, the children know instinctively what their parents really value.

Many parents find this prospect daunting. They know too well how fallible they are. When parents can come together in a cell group they walk the spiritual journey together. Parents and children can admit mistakes and not feel condemned. They can learn from each other.

TO THINK ABOUT

1. Can you think about ideas about God or about yourself which go back to impressions you received in your childhood?

2. Can you identify ideas and opinions which your children hold, and which derive directly from you?

3. Do your children understand when an action is morally wrong? Do they also know that they can be forgiven and restored?

Chapter 14

STAGES OF BELIEF AND DISBELIEF

Many people who have studied the growth of children have used stages of development to describes the growing processes of intellect, moral values, personal relations, emotional growth and even religious understanding.

It is not easy to define specific stages in the spiritual life and of any one child, because they tend to flow into one another and happen at an unequal pace. It depends very much on their environment and how much encouragement they receive from adults. However, there are moments of perception, or times of inner conflict in which they take new truth on board or seek a resolution of ideas. It is helpful to be aware of the signposts, so that we can be aware of the new understanding which the children are experiencing.

STAGES OF FAITH

1. Received Faith
When children are very small, they are not aware that there is any choice to be made. They are born into a religious context, or even an irreligious connect, which they assume is the way the world is. They have never encountered any alternative.

Everything they know about religion has been received, either by word of mouth or by experience. They do what their family does.

For children who are born into a Christian home, God is part of their family – or Jesus. They get a bit confused at first. But he is very real. They talk to him. They talk about him. They know He provides their needs and that they can ask for His help. He is their "Invisible Friend". This is not a strange concept for children. They often develop invisible friends who are very real to them. That is how it is possible for children to form a relationship with God, long before they are capable of putting any facts to their faith.

They derive confidence and support by having Someone who is always there to help them and they quite often talk to Him. Jesus is more than ready to help them. He is completely untroubled by their inability to explain Him. He just opens his arms to receive them and he guards their right to be believers.

If you ask a young child to talk about his/her faith in Jesus, the answer is likely to be, "I love Jesus. Jesus loves me." Or "He's my friend." This very appropriate to their age. It expresses that they have a daily relationship. It may not explain how that relationship came about, or what is the theological basis for it. It is an expression of trust and love, and these are the attitudes that God most desires.

2. Factual Faith
At some time during elementary school a new factor enters the children's thinking. Suddenly they become aware of the world of facts. Until then, there was a wonderful muddle of facts and imagination. Anything could happen.

Chapter 14. Stages of Belief and Disbelief

Suddenly the important question to the children is, "Is this true?" They don't give up on using their imagination, but they want to be clear which things are real and which are not.

At this point children begin to re-examine all they have learned this far, to check it against a standard of "reality." They abandon some of their earlier ideas. Santa Claus is seen as a satisfying tale, which enables the parents to give presents to their children. Older children join the conspiracy of hiding that secret knowledge from the younger children. The tooth fairy is just the excuse for a financial reward. They still enjoy fairy stories, but they do not think fairies are true.

Naturally the children take a fresh look at their Christian faith. They want to know if Jesus is real or just another adult fiction. Is the Bible just a story book? Is there a God who cares, or is he just a legend? Sometimes the picture books they read and the stories they are told, re-inforce the "imaginary" element. The pictures of a cute little ark bobbing around on a deep blue sea, with Mrs Noah hanging out the washing, and an elephant's head sticking out from one end and a giraffe's out the other, makes the event look like a fictional story.

I like to be very specific with children. If a thing is factual I tell them so and I give them the details. If it is fictional, I tell them so but do not let them get mixed up. Some children give up on Jesus because they think he is imaginary, like Santa Claus. The Bible is full of background detail and social background, which can set the stories into their historical setting. The people in the Bible talk like real people and feel in the same way. We recognise their actions and their fears. The more the children can understand them, the more they will believe that these things "really happened."

If you ask children if the stories they hear are true, they will probably say "Yes," because they have learned that everything in the Bible is true. If you ask them, "How do you mean true?" they often say, "Well, there's a lot of truth in them." That isn't quite the same thing. If you ask them, "Did these things really happen?" you often get a different answer.

Often children apply the word "magic" to the miracles of the Bible. That confuses children because they know that magic is a trick or an illusion. They need to understand that God's power is not magic. It is both natural and supernatural. Things we can't explain, happen because of Who He is and because he controls all of creation. He made the laws of nature and he can use them to His purpose.

At this age, children are hungry for detail. That is one reason they like fantasy and computer games. Young children are devoted to dinosaurs and learn bundles of facts about them. If they hear the Bible in the context of the real world, with plenty of facts, the stories become much more interesting.

Children at elementary school are often still rooted in their family home. They accept the family values and they are also asking questions, hundreds of questions. They test our patience and our own world of knowledge. But their questions cannot be brushed off. In their experience, if you don't know, nobody knows. If you don't know the answer to their question, promise them to find out. We have pastors in our churches who are trained to answer questions.

The faith expression of children at this age is often, "I'm of Jesus side." I choose to follow Jesus. They know that there is a choice. They know that their parents follow Jesus and they believe that Jesus loves them and is their leader. They depend

Chapter 14. Stages of Belief and Disbelief

on him daily and they pray for all the crises of a school child. They also try to do a deal with God at times. "If You do this, I'll do that." If they want to do something wrong, they hope God isn't looking. They still have many things to learn but their relationship with God is real.

3. Future Faith

In the higher years of childhood, it dawns upon the children that this Christian faith had long term implications. Until that time, they live very much in the present. The end of each year marks about the limit of their future vision. But as they enter secondary school they have to begin to think of their future direction. They find they are moving into schools away from some of their neighbourhood friends. They have to develop new friends who do not necessarily live close by. The subjects they choose to study at school begin to turn their lives in a specific direction. They lead somewhere. Some children begin to realise that God has a plan about what they might do.

In the High School context, they need to choose whether to make their faith public of private. It's not easy to be a Christian in a school yard. Pre-teens can be loud and bossy about their opinions. Fitting in with the group is a vital factor in socialization. No one wants to be the outcast.

Some young Christians would die rather than admit to their friends that they go to church. One son of a Pastor told his friends, when they asked what his father did, that his father was dead! Another told them that his father was a carpenter. That's getting closer.

One early teenager decided that the only way to survive in school was to make a public declaration of faith and to live with it. She collected plenty of laughter and teasing, but in the end the students recognized that she was O.K. When there was a moral or a spiritual principle issue in the life of the school, she would talk about it to a teacher or the principal, and they would listen to her. They learned to respect her even when they did not agree.

Some parents like to place their children in a Christian school or to Home-School them. I have seen many excellent Christian young people who have been educated this way. It's a good option. But eventually the battle-ground has to be faced. Parents need to make the decision when the time is right for their child to enter the public world. Children learn that being a Christian takes courage and personal commitment. You can't drift into spiritual maturity.

Some children regard their school as a place for outreach. In Singapore we had children who would spend their lunch-break, prayer walking through the school, for the staff and the leaders, for their friends, for their sports and for their exams. They talked to their friends about Jesus and they asked God to bless their school and help them set an example there.

When children have to defend their family faith in the face of peer pressure, they tend to crumble unless they have made that faith their own. If they know God as a personal Friend, who actively share their life experience, when they know they can depend on Him when life gets tough, and when they have a deep inner desire to obey Him and serve Him, they are much more resilient to outside criticism.

The cell group is an ideal place for them to learn their faith and talk about it. As they hear other people's experience they learn how to be brave and yet not aggressive. Their family is not alone.

STAGES OF DISBELIEF

1. One World-view
We have already noted that many young children know of only one world-view. Everyone they know believes the same thing, including grandparents and playmates. They honestly believe that everyone in the world agrees with their family.

When my oldest boy was four, he was watching me dress his little sister who was one.

"I'm on Jesus' side," announced firmly.

"I'm delighted to hear it," I answered.

"But (her name), she's on the Devil's side," he went on.

I raised my eyebrows. 'Why do you say that?' I asked. "Why can't she be on Jesus' side too?"

"But someone's got to be on the Devil's side," he protested. It took me several minutes to explain to him that the Devil had plenty of people on his side without our baby."

It is often quite a shock to the children when they discover their playmates or next-door neighbours belong to another religion.

2. Challenged Faith
The first challenge to the family faith can occur as early as kindergarten, when they discover that many of their new-found friends do not know about Jesus. They ask many questions about it and they firmly believe that their family is right. But a small crack has appeared in their belief system.

They begin to realise that their family may be in the minority. Many other people think differently.

The further they progress through the educational system, the stronger this conflict feels. Their teachers and their close friends may think differently. In the end the child may stand alone. If the child is going to a Christian School, the dissonance is much weaker. They can be glad that they are with a majority. Unfortunately, they sometimes develop a kind of fortress mentality. "We must guard ourselves from the wicked people out there." It makes it harder for the children to integrate with the wider world as they grow.

As school forms a larger and more influential part of a child's life, the children begin to move their authority base. Whereas once Daddy or Mommy knew everything and could be counted on for the right answers, suddenly the school-teacher becomes a new authority. If there is a discussion, the child announces, "But my teacher says…". Often it's not highly charged issue like the creation of the world. It may be the height of the Empire State Building or what made dinosaurs die. Sometimes you will need to explain that there some things that even teachers do not know best.

The higher they rise in the educational system, the more attractive facts and technology become. Children attach themselves to computers as though they were part of their DNA. Soon parents and grandparents will be asking the children for their advice. Scientific discovery and exploration are fascinating for children. The world is so much bigger and smaller than they can see. There are so many wonders that you have to look for. We can't remove our children from the world. They need to live with it.

We should remember that God made the world, He makes it function and He enjoys it. When we discover how things work, we are making a discovery about Him. If we let our children feel that science is the enemy of God, we are creating a dangerous conflict. He does know all about computers. He created the silicon from which they are made. He does understand astronomy and climate and natural history and physics. These are studies of His world and we can walk through His world trusting Him to guide us. When our children meet people who are aggressive and dismissive of Christian faith, we need to be able to enter into the conversation and help our children understand that the true story is far bigger than those people know. They need to hear what God has to say.

Most of all they need to know that the spiritual world is true. The world is not limited to physical and material things. The things that are unseen are more important than the things that are seen and our spiritual relationships will never end.

Children never stop asking questions and seeking for facts. They will say, "Where does God live?" "Is he near or far away" "Is he old or young?" What does He eat? How can He hear everyone's prayers at once?" If you don't know the answers talk to someone who can help you. All these questions show that the children are trying to fit God into the real world. If He stays in their imaginary world, He will lose his significance and power in their lives. We should tell them everything we know about Him.

3. Two Compartment World
If the inner tension between the factual world and the Bible world is not resolved, the children can easily drift into even more dangerous territory. Rather than having to make a choice, the children begin to live in two worlds at once. It is as

though they divide their lives in half. At home and at church they live in a Christian environment and behave in Christian patterns. They know all the right answers and can appear to be regular members of the church community.

At school with their friends, they adopt a secular viewpoint, in which their Christian faith is invisible. They even divide their thinking into two parts. There, Bible knowledge is remote, historic and outdated, while secular knowledge which is fresh, relevant and challenging.

In the church and in the cell group they should be encountering both the Bible and the world around them. We can't close our eyes to the problems in our locality, or in the national and international arena. The children can learn to look with us at what is happening and to listen to what God is saying.

All truth is God's truth wherever it comes from. Mathematics and astronomy are as sacred as theology. It all comes from the beauty and science of God's mind. Similarly, all lies come from the Father of Lies, both lying science and lying religion.

Children can continue living in these two worlds for a long time. Their parents are happy, their friends are happy, their teachers are happy. But eventually, as they grow older, they will have to make a choice. They have ambitions for their lives, and most of their goals appear to be in the secular world. They want a worthwhile career, a place to call home, respect from their peers, a chance to see the world. For them, the church seems to have very little to offer. Few of these children actually reject their faith. They just let it slip away while they do other things.

God does not want His children to have limited prospects of life. If these children choose to follow Him and seek His plan, they can be sure that life will not be boring. God needs Christians of intellectual power in the academic world, innovators and inventors, thinkers and philosophers, news reporters, sports heroes, singers and musicians, doctors and economic wizards, philanthropists and social workers. God wants His children to spread through the world carrying the message of Jesus with them and doing his work wherever they go. There are millions of people whose lives have been fully used and extended and fulfilled, because they answered the call of Jesus.

The children need to meet some of these people to open their eyes to the possibilities. They may be in the cell group or elsewhere in the church Overseas visitors may talk to the children as well as the adults. It maybe through movies or mission trips. The children of our churches need to know what in the world is going on! How can we ever let our children have the idea that the Christian life is small and boring?

4. Breaking Point

Some children finally reach a breaking point with their Christian faith. Sometimes it happens when they go to college. If their Christian life has largely become a habit, it's easy to break in the new environment.

The perceived cause may be very small. An adult makes an unkind criticism; a sports event is scheduled for Sundays. Their friends have other plans and God fades out of their thinking. Their parents are sad and shocked. They hope the break will be temporary and that their early training will bring them back. Sometimes it does, but not till a long empty time has gone by.

The community of the cell group can be a vital help at such a time. Other adult friends can help the parents love the child back into the community. Just knowing that someone is praying is a good memory. They know their cell group members and they can see that their lives are genuine.

The parents also need love and comfort. Often they have tried hard to keep their children and they are ashamed and heartbroken when they turn away. The children do have the right to make an individual choice. Yet God does not give up on the children easily and neither should we.

Sometimes the children never make the choice between the God's world and the secular world. They continue to live in two worlds right through their adult lives and this may be the most tragic place of all. People become comfortable with double standards and double lives. This is the place where Christian testimony breaks down in the clash of the two systems. Others in society look at them and say, "How can a Christian act like that?" It is a betrayal of the Kingdom of God.

TO THINK ABOUT

1. Think back to your early encounters with God. Did you want to follow Him? Did you ever wonder if the Christian faith was true?

2. What are some of the funny questions you have heard children ask about God? Why do they ask such questions?

3. Do you know of any child from a Christian family who has drifted away from God? When did the drift become apparent?

Chapter 15

HOW CHILDREN RECEIVE SALVATION

Most of the children who come to faith in Jesus have had a Christian family, a church or a Christian friend. They learn about Jesus in two ways. First and most important they get to know Christian people and are attracted by their open loving attitudes. They see the way they behave and they are drawn towards their lifestyle and their community. Sometimes children get to know Christians and they are repelled by their life style and their behaviour. This is a tragic outcome because those children have a negative attitude towards God for a long time. All Christians, whether they have children of their own or not, have an absolute responsibility to treat children in the way that Jesus did. He drew children towards Him so that they wanted to share their company.

The second way they get to know about Jesus is by learning about Him from the Bible. Watching Jesus walk in the path of his earthly life, challenges the emerging thinking of the children. Why is Jesus so different from other people I know? That starts a journey of discovery which leads to faith. Whatever else Jesus was, no one could ever say He was boring. That is why we must not make Him seem boring to children when they are in study groups. We need to convey our own passion and excitement for him, in the way we tell the stories.

It is important for children to synchronise the message they hear from the Bible with the message they receive for the people of the faith community. This is the acid test of the Gospel. If it doesn't work in the lives of people today, it doesn't work regardless of what happened two thousand years ago.

Intergenerational cells can fill in the missing dimension in children's evangelism. In the cell group church children receive Bible teaching each week, but it is supported and validated each week in the cell group where the children experience the life of the body of Christ.

On the negative side, some children who are born into Christian homes may receive Bible teaching at home, in the church and in school. Yet as soon as they can they turn away. This is the hardest group of people to reach because they think they know the church. The president of the Atheist's Society in my university was the son of a good Baptist family. He knew the Gospel but turned away in disgust at what he saw happen in the church.

Some people give the impression that, unless a young person has sown his wild oats during his teens, he must be a very dull person, with no spark or drive. I don't accept that. Why should our children have to go through a period of trouble and rebellion just to prove that they are "fun people?"

One day my son, then in his early twenties, said to me, "Mum, I have to give my testimony in church, but I don't know what to say. My testimony's so boring. I've never done anything sensational. I've never been on drugs. I've never been drunk. I've gone to church all my life and followed Jesus the best way I can. I haven't got anything to say."

I turned to him. "I don't think you have a dull testimony. You are a good news story. You didn't go out and damage someone else's life, trying to have a good time. Jesus has kept you safe through lots of adventures, like when you were stranded in Japan without money. You've used your talents in music and you trusted God to help you overcome your physical disability. That's not boring. That's a triumph!"

"Go out there and tell the people about your great God. Tell them they can overcome temptation and still enjoy life. Tell them that God can see you through when things get really tough." So he did.

BRINGING A CHILD TO THE POINT OF DECISION

When you lead a child to receive Jesus into their lives, you are forming a relationship with them, even if that is the first time you have met. We cannot introduce them to Him and then walk off and leave them. Nurturing a new baby is as important as bringing it into the world.

I remember seeing a child of eleven lead a child of six to Christ. She did a good job and the little girl understood the decision she was making. At the end of the conversation the little girl hugged her new friend and asked, "I will see you again won't I?" A new relationship had begun.

THE STEPS OF A FAITH DECISION.

There are various booklets which outline the steps a child might make in entering a new friendship with Jesus. I've written one myself, called "Breaking the Barrier." It is a picture sticker book, which is a great advantage because the children quickly learn to use it themselves to explain their faith to others.

These are the steps which are covered.

1. God loves every person in the world. Including you and me. He likes us so much that He wants us to be with Him forever.

2. People want to do what they like and to be bad if they want to. We all do that, including you and me. That means we cannot be with Him forever because He is totally good.

3. There is no way we can get back to God by ourselves. We can never be good enough by ourselves. Going to church is not enough. There is only one way and that is through Jesus.

4. How does that work? God knew that people could not find their way back to Him by themselves so He sent Jesus, His own Son, into our world. People hated Him because he was good, so they killed him even though he had done nothing bad. He died for us. When he died there was a gap in the Sin Barrier. He stands in our place and we can get back to God through Him. If we become friends of Jesus, God will forgive us for the bad things we have done for His sake. Now we can live with God forever. He will always be our Friend.

Then you ask if the child would like to follow Jesus and be His friend. Help the child to tell Him so in his own words.

Prayer: Thank you Jesus for dying for me so that I can get back to God. Please forgive me for the bad things I have done and thought. Forgive me for not wanting You to be in my life.

From now on I want to follow you for the rest of my life and live with You forever. Amen"

Read the verse, John 3:16 with the child, making it personal by replacing the word "whosoever" with the child's name. If he/she can memorise the verse, it will remind them that if anyone believes he will have eternal life, starting today.

MUDDLED PICTURES OF SALVATION

It isn't hard to lead children to follow Jesus. It's much harder to be sure that the children understand what has happened. Many adults forget that children do not understand metaphors or theological ideas. They present the message in language which confuses the children and leaves them with a very odd view of what they have just decided. Some salvation booklets have the same problem. Just writing hard words in block capital letters does not make them any easier to understand.

The worst trap is the use of "heart" language. Christians use the word "heart as a metaphor for a person's whole life and experience – their mind, their feelings, their will.

Unfortunately, children do not understand it this way. They imagine that Jesus miniaturises Himself and enters the cavities of our physical heart. One little boy said to his mother, "Mommy, you know how I asked Jesus into my heart last Sunday? Well, could you tell Him to come out because He's too big for me and He hurts."

Another child who was feeling sick, threw up his meal and exclaimed,

"Whoops! I just lost Jesus."

Another boy came home from Sunday School and said to his mother, "Mom, I gave my heart to Jesus today."

"That's wonderful," she answered, giving him a hug.

"But Mommy, will it hurt?"

Then his mother discovered that he believed he had agreed to have a heart transplant so he could give his heart to Jesus. No wonder he felt worried.

Even visual illustrations of salvation often give a wrong impression. One child from outside the church, woke up screaming, because she had seen an illustration of a stylized heart filled with creepy, crawly sins. She thought she was infested. Some children thought their hearts had literally turned black and they needed to have it scrubbed white. This is a very unpopular idea among the darker nations of the world.

Many children will say, "Yes, I love Jesus" but they do not know that they are pledging to obey and follow Him every day. They think they are making an arrangement to get into heaven but they do not know that it will affect their daily behaviour.

In some nations the children may not know that they are choosing to follow Jesus only. They are happy to add Jesus to their list of Gods. One girl was telling her mother that she had decided to follow Jesus. Her mother showed great alarm, because their family were Buddhists. "That's O.K," said the girl. "I love Jesus and I love Buddha too. I can love both."

God is very gracious in understanding how children think and feel, even if their ideas are primitive. He accepts the

Chapter 15. How Children Receive Salvation

level of faith they offer. However they do need a friend to walk alongside them to explain more about the faith they are entering.

DO THE DECISIONS OF THE VERY YOUNG MEAN ANYTHING?

Some educators doubt whether children can have a valid experience of faith before they can fully understand what it means. We need to remember that entry into the Kingdom of Heaven is based on relationship, not intellectual understanding. Therefore a child who is capable of relating to another person and can conceive the idea of a loving invisible Divine Friend, can start a relationship with Him. When a small child says, "I love Jesus and Jesus loves me," that is a valid relationship for his/her age.

Later on as he starts making choices and understands more, he may phrase his faith differently. "I want to follow Jesus. I want to be His friend." As they begin to understand that following Jesus is a life commitment, they will express it more at this level. "I choose Jesus to be my leader. He will be the Lord of my life and I will obey Him."

A child of three cannot make a life commitment for a child of thirteen or an adult of thirty. Their initial love sets the direction and their decision grows as their understanding grows. This is sometimes confusing to caring parents who see their children make multiple decisions to become a Christian as they are growing up. They need not worry. The initial decision is just stretching and growing as they mature and understand more. My friend, Dr Ralph Neighbour, explains it this way. "When we are young we are saying to God, "All I know about me, I give to all I know about You." At that age the child does not know a great deal about himself of God. But as he learns more, he keeps on saying, "All that I know about me, I give to all I know about You." At each stage of life, it is a bigger decision and it stays with us all through life. In our old age we are still saying, "All I know about me now, I still give to all I know about You" And I am still saying it at the age of eighty.

Faith is never static and set in concrete. The newborn baby grows and matures and eventually grows old. So also it is with the second birth.

ANXIOUS PARENTS

Often anxious parents try to elicit a verbal decision from their children at a very young age. If the children do no more than assent to what Mommy and Daddy are saying, the child's decision may be ineffective. Children may try to continue to meet their parent's expectations and win their approval without ever having entered into a personal relationship with Jesus. This lack often becomes all too obvious when the pressure comes on in teen-age years.

One mother instructed he daughter one day, "Now that you're eight years old, dear, it's time you got saved. So when the Preacher gives the invitation, you go forward and get saved." When I met this woman later as a grown woman, she had long since rejected the decision she felt was forced upon her.

Much of this anxiety in parents arises from the fear that their children will die without receiving Christ. They forget that God is not willing that one of these little ones should perish.[63] They have not read the word in I Corinthians 7:14 in which

---

63. Matthew 18:14

God assures us that the children of believers are holy even if only one parent is a believer.

This does not mean that parents should not attempt to lead their children into a relationship with Jesus. Rather they should talk about Jesus in their daily life. Tell them how they came to know Jesus. Help the children to include Jesus as the most important Person in their life and their best Friend.

Many Christian people cannot tell the day on which they first received Jesus into their lives. They walked with Him in infancy, childhood and right up to the present moment and their present experience of Him is real. For children from Christian homes this is a most healthy and genuine experience. Sometimes they feel embarrassed when other people try to make them name a day.

TO THINK ABOUT

1. Have you ever helped a child to follow Jesus? How well did the child understand what you said? Did the child ask questions? Were you able to continue the relationship?

2. How old were you when you first received Christ? Can you remember what you felt at the time? Was it the beginning of a change in your life?

3. Have you been part of an event in which larger numbers of children were led to Jesus? Was there any attempt to follow them up afterwards? Were there any lasting relationships formed? Do you know some who are still practising their faith now?

Chapter 16

NURTURING AND MENTORING

THE ADVANTAGES OF A CHRISTIAN HOME

Children who have grown up in a Christian home have undoubted advantages as they set out of their Christian life. They have heard stories about Jesus from their earliest years. Often they have lived with parents whose lives and words speak of Jesus. Their lives are good examples. They will probably have been part of a church community where they have had a chance to see other Christians and form some positive relationships with them.

It is a very welcome event when the child decides to express their own faith in Jesus. Their parents and grandparents will be delighted. There may be a celebration or a special gift to mark the occasion. Friends at school may not be impressed, but they know that this child comes from an "odd religious" family.

Already these children have a value system instilled by their family practices. They know it is not right to steal or tell lies, or cheat or swear. They are used to people praying from time to time especially when things go wrong. They have already been going to church regularly and they know how to behave there and they have quite a bit of Bible knowledge. In short, they don't have to make too many obvious changes when they start to live seriously as Christians.

THE DOWNSIDE OF A CHRISTIAN BACKGROUND

Most of these children know that following Jesus ought to produce that some positive changes in their lives but being honest, they cannot see much difference. Often they wonder if they ever received Jesus at all. Perhaps they didn't get the words right?

Some children make up the deficiency by making up a spectacular testimony. One girl of about ten told how she had been lost in sin and degradation. She had broken every commandment and was a rebel against God. However, when she was saved at the age of five (!) her life totally changed and she was able to live a life of holiness.

A good friend who is mentoring the child, can help her to overcome the dis-satisfaction she may feel with her own Christian life. She shouldn't be pressured into faking "sins" and precocious "holiness" out of a desire to please the people around her. She will be helped by someone who shares honest conversations about her daily life and experience. Christian development can seem very slow to a child at this time, who would much rather experience something dramatic.

Every child needs to have a period of following through on his/her faith decision. The basic facts of salvation and continuing Christian life need to be spelled out to the child with plenty of chances for discussion and clarification. My discipling book is called, "Now I Follow Jesus." It is still in

Chapter 16. Nurturing and Mentoring

print and available in Singapore.[64] It covers topics of "Who is my New Friend," "Prayer, "The Holy Spirit" " Obeying God" "Witnessing" "Temptations and Forgiveness." Other similar books may also be excellent.

If a mentor is discussing these issues with a child or children, it should be over a set period of time with opportunity for discussion and practical assignments which the children can report on. Learning a new life cannot happen just by reading out of a book.

Introducing the children to a prayer life is like giving breathing apparatus to a new baby. If the new believer is getting to know a new Friend, he/she needs to be able to talk to Him and listen to Him. Talking to God and finding that he is real is the first proof that Jesus is close by and will always be there to help and comfort.

The other vital Friend they need to know about is the Holy Spirit. Their concept of the Trinity may be fairly basic, but when they know the Holy Spirit, they will have access to power and encouragement, which is available even to children. The Holy Spirit dwells in every believer, children included and they need to be aware of their mighty Friend.

When you listen to the testimonies of teen-agers you find they tend to downgrade their childhood faith experience. They will say something like this.

"I was brought up in a Christian home, so I became a Christian when I was quite young, but it didn't mean much to me until last weekend when I went to the youth camp. I suddenly discovered the reality I've always been looking for. I received

---

64. Growing Families International dorcas.li@gfi-singapore.org

the Holy Spirit and it was just wonderful and now I'm praising Jesus. I suppose when I was young I received Jesus as Savior but I now I've received Him as Lord."

I'm not sure that it's possible for anyone to receive Jesus as Savior and not to obey Him and follow Him as Lord. What seems to have really happened is that a child was willing to make a "decision" because it was asked of him/her, but there was no discipling or nurturing so that the child could grow into mature faith according to their age.

No one expects a child to grow up into maturity and understanding overnight. But they should be growing into a faith which is mature for their age-group. In many church situations the child's decision faith decision is recorded as though It was an end in itself. The child is put on hold for six or seven years until a later more meaningful decision can be attained. Our children should not be allowed to imagine that their faith decision has brought them a ticket to heaven and the serious stuff comes later. Neither should the church think that way.

Real faith in the hearts of children produces real obedience and willingness to know Jesus better. Discipleship is not an option, even for children.

That is why our church in Singapore, Faith Community Baptist Church, planned and developed an Equipping Track to lead the children from the point of decision to full, active, obedient and reproducing Christian life, before they entered teen-age years. It was one of the best things we did. They entered the Youth Ministry on track to become leaders and helpers among their peers.

NO REPENTANCE, NO GRATITUDE

When I was a young baptised Christian, around the age of eleven or twelve, I sometimes had a problem trying to compare my experience of faith with the things I heard from adults and older teens. I knew that it is vital that we repent from our sins and ask for God's forgiveness.

Sometimes in our youth group we would pray round the room with each person confessing their sins and asking forgiveness. I can remember dreading the moment when my turn came, because I couldn't think what to say. At that time, dancing was about the worst sin I could think of. I had never been to a dance, but I confessed to "wanting" to dance, and asked forgiveness for that. In my "good girl" role I had never identified some of the ugly things in my life, my sense of superiority, my catty remarks about other people, my glossy excuses to cover up any weaknesses in my behaviour. I certainly had things I could have confessed, but at that time I couldn't identify them.

Because I had never truly recognised the things that were wrong in my life, I never experienced the joy of forgiveness. Though I knew Jesus loved and died for me, I never felt the overflowing burst of gratitude of knowing His lovingkindness and cleansing. I suspect that this is a flaw in many of our church kids. They know they are right and they feel rather smug about it.

Jesus once said "He who has been forgiven little, loves little, and he who has been forgiven much, loves much." That is why many children find it hard to worship. Worship is based on a sense of closeness to God and a strong sense of gratitude to Him.

My daughter once told me when she was about thirteen, she thought God ought to be fairly pleased with her because she had decided to follow Him. She could have run away from home or got into drugs or alcohol or illicit sex. But instead she had been faithful to God and kind to her parents and had not given anyone any worry. She hoped God appreciated that. Her inner heart was saying, "God, I thank you that I am not like other girls, chasing boys, getting drunk, or high on drugs and staying out all hours of the night. – or even like this tax-collector!"

It is such a fine line between being good and obedient and being a young Pharisee. Now there's something we can repent about. It is true that God loves his beautiful faith children with all His heart and His heart almost bursts with pleasure when He thinks about all the potential they have now and in the future. But His heart almost breaks when he sees them harden into the pride of religion when He cannot use them anymore. Children need to understand how much their Father loves them, how much Jesus did to give them a chance of salvation. They need to feel the quickening touch of the Holy Spirit to see the world through His eyes and to love it for His sake. This is the reality which is life-changing and it comes from deep love and not mere words.

WHAT IS THE WORLD LIKE?

The other disadvantage for children from Christian homes and churches is that they have very little idea of what the world is like outside their area of experience. We have tried to guard them from the dangers of the world. They know that people in the world are supposed to be miserable, but it sure looks like they have fun.

Chapter 16. Nurturing and Mentoring

When they become independent at the time when they leave home or go to College, they suddenly have the chance to try out some of those forbidden things. They don't intend to turn their back on their faith or on the church, but as they drift along they suddenly find that they don't want to go back. They've gone too far.

Sheltering children from the traps of world is often a fruitless exercise. If you forbid an undesirable television or game, they will watch it at a friend's place. If you warn against a bad friendship, it suddenly becomes a lot more attractive.

The only real way to satisfy a child's natural curiosity is to help them evaluate what they see and make good decisions for themselves. If you watch television together and talk about it, they will know why some programs have negative messages and low values. They need to be able to see the mindset that lies behind the media. If they've already been able to make good choices, they will continue to make them when they are on their own.

One boy was keen on watching "Power Rangers" on television but his mother was uneasy about the program. At last she said, "Why don't we watch "Power Rangers" together and we'll invite Jesus to watch it with us. At the end of the show she said, "Well what did you think?"

"It was great," he replied.

"What did Jesus think?" she asked him.

He paused a minute and said, "I'll ask Him." In a few minutes his head bobbed up. "Jesus said that He liked it and He didn't like it."

"What does that mean?" asked his mother.

"Jesus liked it because they were fighting evil, but He didn't like it because they were using the power of animals and not God's power."

We need to trust our children to think about things and make good decisions.

We can listen to them and help them to think deeper. But there will be moments when they are on their own and have to make a choice.

Narelle, who lives in Australia, had been taught the dangers of calling up spirits through ouija boards. She arrived late at a friend's birthday party to discover all her friends were gathered around playing with a ouija board. They called her to hurry and join in the fun, but she refused.

"Come on," they said. "Don"t be scared. It's great fun and it really works."

"Not while I'm here," said Narelle. "The Holy Spirit lives in me and he is stronger than any evil spirit."

"Don't be silly," they urged. "It's just a game."

Narelle just went off to a corner and found a magazine, but inside she was praying. From that moment the oiuja board became lifeless. The could get no response. Before long they gave up and played something else.

There are many games and movies which dabble in the occult – tarot cards, swinging gold rings, fortune telling etc. They are very attractive until the children have learned the power that lies behind them.

HOW MUCH DO OUR CHILDREN NEED TO KNOW?

You do not need to experience sin-traps to discover what they are like. It is much better if children find out how ugly and miserable are the temptations of the world, while they are still within the protection of the family.

One night our family was camping in the city of Amsterdam. Their father and I talked about how much of Amsterdam we should allow our teenagers to see. After a discussion, we all went out just after dark and walked together through the red light area of the city. Then we returned to our campervan and talked about we had seen. Our children were shocked. Our daughter was angry and indignant that girls would dress up and sell themselves like merchandise. Our oldest son observed their gray faces and the pinpricks on their arms. Our youngest son decided that it was all "Yukky."

Then we talked about the pressures of life which had brought them to this situation, the drugs and the debts and the pimps who exploit the girls. It was a graphic lesson on the darker side of life and they did not have to escape from us, to find out for themselves. They also learned to thank God for their salvation and to care about the people who were caught in the bitter trap.

CHILDREN FROM NON-CHURCH HOMES

When children from outside the church culture decide to follow Jesus, they face a very different response. Their families do not welcome the news. How could they? Suddenly the child is choosing a faith which is different from what they have been taught.

The parents' fear are very natural. Is their child really old enough to make such a decision? Are they going through a religious phase? Will the church try to divide the family? Are they getting into some dangerous cult? Will their children get awkward and refuse to do what the family wants?

For this reason, I very seldom recommend that the children be sent home to announce that they have decided to follow Jesus. The parents do not know what that means. They may imagine a group of narrow-minded people, who will try to crush their child's opportunities or talents. The children do not know how to explain what has happened to them. They use wrong descriptions which often frighten or anger the parents.

Instead I tell children that when they go home, Jesus will go with them. He will tell them how to behave in their families and do the things He wants them to do. I say, "Let's see how long it will be before your parents see any difference in you. When they ask how you have change, then tell them that you are trying to follow Jesus and be obedient."

Meanwhile I try to get to visit the parents and tell them how much we have enjoyed getting to know their child. They have much to be thankful for in having such a friendly and polite child, and we felt we should meet his/her parents. I would explain that we have a group of families meeting nearby, and we would love to have the child continuing to meet with us. The parents would also be very welcome to come and see for themselves. Most families are open to a friendly approach, where they can meet the people who are sharing in their children's lives.

Chapter 16. Nurturing and Mentoring

Even if they say "No", we can ask if we may invite the children to special social events as they arise.

If the children are permitted to attend the cell group, one family or adult should choose to act as a sponsor for the child. They would be like "god-parents." They would make sure of the child's safety, oversee his/her behaviour, lead them in discipleship and make friends with his/her parents. Sometimes he would be able to visit the home of his sponsors.

In one of our cell groups, four children from the apartment building turned up one night when we were having a celebration. With their parents' permission they continued to attend the cell group and they received Christ. About eight months later, the cell group was having another "harvest event." The first person to arrive was the father of these children. He said to the cell leader, "I want to know what you do with my children here. They have been so much better since they started coming to your group. They talk about Jesus all the time. If your Jesus can be so good for my children, perhaps He can be good for me too."

He received Christ that night and his wife did so a few days later.

TOO MANY CHILDREN

Sometimes there will be a sudden influx of new believer children. This is very exciting but they can also dominate the cell group. Sometimes two or three of the adult cell members can form a sub-group to welcome the children and start them on the first stages of their Christian life. The sub-group is still part of the mother cell, and it is hoped that the parents will in time become part of the cell group. If they all come from one neighbourhood, the mother cell group might plant a new cell group in the area to include the new families.

A useful, but less effective option is to have an "Echoes" day or a Day Camp when the new believing children are gathered together to remember what happened. You can confirm their faith and set them on the first steps of discipleship. The aim is to continue the friendship with the child so they know they have not been forgotten.

Sometimes children from non-Christian homes face stiff opposition to their faith. They do have a few advantages too. Because they are in a resistant environment, they can become very strong and clear in their faith. A girl in Singapore told us that her mother forced her to her knees so that she would worship the family idols. She said that while her family were praying, she was silently saying to Jesus, "I'm not really worshipping these idols. I'm really worshipping You."

God seems to give special strength to children who do not receive encouragement in their homes. In New Zealand I met a boy during the Bible class in his school. He waited to talk to me after school one day to ask if he could be a Christian. As soon as I explained the choice, he gladly decided to follow Jesus from now on. I found a simple Bible for him and I taught him how to pray.

At the beginning of next term his family had moved to another area and I never saw him again. However almost two years later I was talking to a Presbyterian lady at an inter-church function. She asked if I knew this boy. It seems their church had been visiting lapsed members and they arrived at his home. His parents quickly said that they had no further interest in the church, but the boy spoke up. "I'm a Christian. Can I go to church?" His parents were amazed, but they agreed to let him go to church if he wanted to. God held that boy's faith for two years before He found someone to help him.

This story does not mean that we can neglect discipling children. It shows that God's grace is so great to his little ones, that He will be their spiritual Father if they have no-one else.

One of the delights of working with these children is that they have no prior knowledge of the Bible. They are hearing it all for the first time and they ask wonderful questions. For them it is like a new world, good and exciting and very real. They can see that the people they meet in the cell group are different and real too. They should be a good advertisement for the Gospel of Jesus.

Sometimes children who have grown up in the church environment, can "freeze" out a newcomer. They show off their Bible knowledge and laugh at that questions a child may ask. This isolates the new child and makes it hard for him/her to belong. We need to train our church children to welcome new children and not embarrass them. Once they can begin to help them and pray for them, children can actually help sponsor the newcomers and be their protectors.

All children need someone to walk beside them as they take the first steps of the Christian journey. With love and encouragement from the cell group community, their first faith decision can become a choice which lasts them all their lives.

TO THINK ABOUT

Has this chapter reminded you of things you have seen happen in the lives of children you know, or perhaps even your own life? How can we help children grow into sensible mature young Christians?

How do you think parents should protect their children from the evil pressures in their society?

How can we help children understand how much God loves them and has done for them so that they learn to love and thank Him too?

Chapter 17

AN EQUIPPING TRACK FOR CHILDREN

If we are serious about leading our children into spiritual maturity and ministry, we need a systematic way of doing it. We need to decide the goals we are aiming at and find reachable ways for the children to achieve them at their own age-level. The aim in not just to have a highly Biblically literate echelon of children.

We want the children to experience what real Christian life is all about – the walk of faith; the power of prayer; the joy of worship; the call to witness; the challenge of learning; the daily presence of the Holy Spirit. Once they have proved the power and presence of God in their ordinary lives, it is much harder from them to turn their backs on Him.

Church is not play-school for children. It is equipping children for life and mobilizing them for ministry. After a time, the Youth ministry at Faith Community Baptist Church began to report that the children who had been recently promoted to the Youth Department were already keen and ready to learn the skills of serving their high school peers.

The Equipping Track should not be just a church-based course. Parents are at the heart of it and often they make the best sponsors for the children. They can be available to the children every day and they have good experience of their own growing in Christ to share with the children. It is important for the children to hear how their parents came to know Jesus. Parental sponsorship does not happen haphazardly. They need to be aware of what they are trying to do. Many parents feel grossly inadequate for their task of spiritual leadership especially in the hurly burly of family life. They would rather that some expert from the church would do it. But that misses the spiritual bonding which takes place when a family is walking the Christian journey together.

Even if the parents are new Christians themselves, they can draw on the help of other cell members and their own sponsors to learn how to equip their children.

If a child does not have Christian parents, they need another friend to be their sponsor and friend, to answer their questions, to encourage them in difficulties and to show them what God's lovingkindness is like. Their sponsor should also get to know their family and show themselves to be friends and allies.

THE EQUIPPING TRACK FRAMEWORK.

The Equipping Track is a series of stages of spiritual development which take place over an elastic period of time, and that do not come to a fixed conclusion. Some stages may be happening at the same time, as the children grow in different areas of life. The children do not cease to practise these skills once they have reached a level of understanding. They are life-skills which will stay with them forever.

Chapter 17. An Equipment Track for Children

The stages do not have to be completed in a set time and there is no graduation. Everything they learn is open-ended with further knowledge and experience lying ahead. At the age of eighty, I am still making new discoveries about God's kingdom and the way He wants us to participate in it. Children progress at different speeds, according to their age and their ability to share in it. But we love to see that all the children are growing. Recognising that the process is ongoing and free-flowing, we need to mark the landmarks of the stages.

Stage 1:
1. Point of Decision

The children may have been growing in their spiritual life before this but sometime there comes a moment when they clearly choose to follow Jesus. It may be expressed in a number of ways and it may happen over a period of time, but at the end they accept who Jesus is and what He has done and they choose to follow and obey Him.

Sometimes this can be a special event where someone leads them through a faith process using a salvation booklet. Sometimes it can be significant conversation. Sometimes it can happen in the midst of a message or presentation, or sometimes it is a personal expression of faith to a parent or a very close friend.

It should involve a moment of prayer when the child tells Jesus what they are deciding to do, asking for his forgiveness and thanking Him for His love. They should feel that they have been accepted into God's Kingdom.

It is often good to have a book to outline what their decision means. It is something for them to keep so that if they start to have second thoughts, they can go back and check out again what it was all about. My book, "Breaking the Barrier" is helpful because it is interactive and it helps the children understand how salvation works.

Stage 1:
2. The Journey Guide

At our church in Singapore we developed a sort of Map which showed the children the steps in the journey as new Christians. It showed them where they were now at the beginning of the journey and guided them through the faith landmarks they would pass as they grew up spiritually.

Many of the children kept "The Journey Guide" for a long time so they could check the steps as they were completed. Their answers at a later age showed significant growth in maturity.

It is also a diagnosis tool to reveal any hidden problems which the children may be facing, especially fears or misunderstandings they may have picked up on the journey so far.

One mother told that as she was reading "The Journey Guide" with her daughter she was shocked at a reaction which she had never suspected. They had been talking about how much God loves her, in the same way that her parents love her. Her comment was, "Well, I know that you and Daddy love me, but I don't think believe God loves me." Her mother was horrified. They had taught her about God's love from the time she was tiny. "Why don't you believe that God loves you?" she asked.

"If God loves me," said the girl, "He wouldn't have made me so ugly." It seems that her friends at school had been telling her she was ugly, and when she looked in the mirror she agreed with them.

There are many things happening in a child's life which are not immediately obvious. Often they can prevent the child from developing a natural loving relationship with God. It may be fear, or bad dreams, or peer pressure, or low self-esteem, or shame over some failure or unpopularity or envy or social embarrassment It is a real help if the children can have an honest talking relationship with a family member or friend to let some of these things come to light.

Stage 1:
3. Basic Discipling

Children need to discover what their new life is all about. Even children who have grown up in the church do not always understand the implications of following Jesus. In my discipling book ("Now I Follow Jesus") I tried to create a shared experience for children and their parent/sponsors. It is an easy book for the parents to handle with cartoon characters asking the awkward questions.

The most important part of the book is at the end of each chapter, when the children are encouraged to ask their parents questions about their own Christian walk. E.g. "When did you become a Christian, Mommy?" or "What are some of the things you pray about, Daddy?" Some children have never heard the story of how their parents came to discover Jesus. Some parents find this quite threatening, but many parents are delighted that they are able to have a spiritual conversation with their children for the first time.[65]

---

[65]. I think this book is still available through Dorcas Li dorcas.li@gfi-singapore.org Other similar books may be more available in your area.

Stage 1:
4. Daily Time With God

As the children start out on their journey we like them to set up a time of talking and listening with God each day. We devised for them a daily Bible reading book based on the book of Mark., called "Treasure Hunt with Mark." There were two age levels, 5-8 years and 9-12 years. Mark is the tour guide and they find the treasure as they read through the Gospel. There is a chart to fill in so they can watch their own progress.

The children can often work their way through this book by themselves, but often the parents encourage them and answer questions. If the child does not have a simple Bible or New Testament at home, the sponsor should make it a special gift.

The daily prayer which arises from these notes is a vital part. One of the most important things we can do for new young believers is to help them to pray. They can always reach God in their daily difficulties even when a parent or sponsor is not there. When they discover that He hears them and answers them, they discover His reality.

Stage 2 of the Equipping Track:
1. Cell Group Participation.

As soon as possible after a child has decided to follow Jesus, we tried to connect them with an Intergenerational Cell Group. Often they were already in a cell group and then the whole cell group will celebrate the new birth of a young believer. If they did not already belong to a cell group we would try to link them (and their family) to a group where they would l feel at home and welcome.

Chapter 17. An Equipment Track for Children

If the children could not belong to a cell group, we tried to find them a small community of other Christians. It might be a Sunday cell group at the church, or a weekday cell group in the neighbourhood. Some members of an intergenerational cell might lead it. Sometimes a family would invite the child into their home to get to know their family and to act as sponsors to the child.

Stage 2:
2. Christian Family Values.

Many Christian families like to have a family worship and prayer time during the week. This gives the family a chance to share what is happening in their lives and to talk about some of the questions they may be facing. I have a written a book called, "The Family Journeys Together" which may be used for this purpose. It is not a study book. It is a collection of interactive experiences which use games and family situations to teach Christian values. Parents are the best people to teach Christian values because they live in the place where the family values show.

It is amazing how children who have sincerely believed in Jesus, can continue to carry sub-Christian values and behaviour into their lives. Selfishness, anger, lying, malice, bullying or hypocrisy can continue to exist, undetected in a child's life especially if they see their peers practising these things around them. One little boy said to me doubtfully one day, "If I believe in Jesus, does that mean that I can't be naughty anymore?" I think he thought that was too much to pay.

Of course none of us can claim to lead a perfect life after salvation. We have to recognise what we have done wrong, and ask for forgiveness. Sometimes we also have to set it right with other people. The children need to know that all of offences can be removed if we ask Jesus to clean us up – again!

Some children think that if you sin after you have decided to follow Jesus, then you need to be saved all over again. They can learn how gracious and forgiving God really is and how much He wants us to succeed. They also learn that adults also have to ask for forgiveness sometimes and set things right.

In the family the children learn how to make good choices and they may also learn the results of making bad choices. Some of the topics that could be discussed are sibling rivalry, schoolyard pressures, playing fair in games, not cheating in exams, not using or abusing other people's possessions, but being kind to weaker or lonely children. Sometimes parents may need to talk about serious things like the use of money, the pressure of work and family life, family confidences, or asking for help when it is needed.

It is so good for children to know and see what a happy marriage is like, what marriage vows are about and how to keep them. Sometimes they even need to know how to handle conflict in the family and who could be a safe friend.

One of the purposes of a family cell group is to let the family have fun together. Family worship should not be so strict and serious that the children hate it and try to avoid it. It's a relational time when the family can learn and laugh together.

Some children do not have the opportunity to share in a family group at home. For these children we devised a book on Christian values which could be used by children on their own. It was called "Living Life Upside Down." Ideally they would still need a sponsor to help with their questions and to encourage them to keep going.

Stage 2
3. Understanding and Sharing the Lord's Supper

In the Intergenerational Cell Group the children will experience the Lord's Supper up close. If they are truly following Jesus they will want to participate. There are two requirements for people to be able to share in the Lord's Supper. They need to have committed themselves to love and follow Jesus and they need to understand the meaning of the symbols of the bread and the cup.

The cell group is a great place for children to learn what the Lord's Supper means. Their parents and friends can show them what happens and explain how they feel about it. Often children are served first by their father or mother. It doesn't seem to matter if some children partake and some do not. The children come with a sense of awe and if they know they do not follow Jesus, they do not want to partake. I remember overhearing one little girl say to her sister, "You don't just take it because you're hungry. You only take it if you love Jesus."

Some people ask what would happen if a child took the Lord's Supper and then lost their faith later in life. I do not see why this question applies only to children. Adults are just as capable of losing their faith or betraying their Lord. Haven't we all dropped back at times from our highest moments of faith and fervour?

Many children I know approach the Lord's Supper in deep sincerity. For children who come from non-church homes the ceremony is of great significance. They regard it as a high privilege to be able to share it. If any child should approach with a wrong attitude, it is easy in the cell group to gently set it right. We adults need to remember that we do not come to His table because of our maturity and holiness but because of His love and our need for forgiveness. It is the "Family Meal" of the Kingdom. When the Holy Spirit stirs up a young believer's heart so they want to share in the Lord's supper, we do not have the right to refuse them.

Stage 2:
Sharing the Gospel

Because it was the practice at Faith Community Baptist Church to teach every new believer in Jesus to share the Gospel with their friends and neighbours, it was natural to teach the children to do it too. Our faith decision booklet, "Breaking the Barrier made it easy for the children because the visuals were brightly coloured and they came in the form of stickers. As you place the stickers on the diagram, the Gospel story became clear.

We would start by letting the children practise in twos in the cell groups. The older children could help the younger ones. They learned how to use the book but they were not considered to have completed this stage until they had shared the booklet with someone who was not a Christian. It was such an exciting moment when they had shared the Gospel story and someone had accepted it.

I know how they felt. When I was eleven years old I first led a friend to Jesus. It wasn't something I wanted to do. I had a close friend who had brought four of her school friends to a children's church camp. One of the girls was called "Annette" and made a claim to be the special friend of my friend so that she squeezed me out. I was angry and jealous and moped around wishing Annette was not there.

Chapter 17. An Equipment Track for Children

One wet afternoon Annette asked if she could climb on my bunk and ask me something. Grudgingly I said she could. To my total surprise she asked what it meant to be a Christian. My first thought was "Oh No! Surely she's not going to be in heaven too!" However, my conscience came to the surface and reluctantly I began to tell her how Jesus died for us all, and for her. I expected her to laugh at me but to my amazement she asked if she could become a Christian. Very simply she received Jesus as her Savior.

Her attitude in the camp was immediately transformed. She kept saying, "I never understood it before. Now I can see what it all means." My attitude was also transformed. Suddenly I saw her through new eyes- someone who was discovering Jesus for the first time. That experience changed my life. It was so exciting I want it to happen over and over again.

Children are very natural and direct when they start to tell someone about Jesus. In Virginia, USA a father told me about his nine-year-old daughter. She was attending their cell group regularly. One of the members had brought along a friend, a burly non-Christian man in his forties. All the adults were making him feel welcome and trying hard not to embarrass him.

The girl found herself sitting beside him, so she turned to him and asked directly. "Sir, are you a Christian?"

He shuffled a little and said, "No, I guess I'd have to say I'm not a Christian."

"Would like to be a Christian?" asked the girl.

"Well, sure," he said.

"I can show you how," the girl replied. And she did. Right in front of the whole cell group. The man not only received Jesus but a year later he was leading his own cell group.

I would like every child in the Kingdom to have that kind of experience. If it happens in childhood, it becomes part of their Christian life-style.

Stage 3 of the Equipping Track
1. Spiritual Formation

Spiritual Formation classes are available to older children as the need arises. Often they are scheduled because a number of children have been enquiring about baptism. In a cell group, a child may ask for baptism when they see other cell members being baptised. That parents will discuss it with the cell leaders and if they think the child is hearing God's call to baptism, they will recommend as a group that the child should be included in the next Spiritual Formation classes.

The classes were led by some Children's Ministry staff, over a period of two weekends. Even though the parents did not lead the Spiritual Formation, we strongly encouraged them to attend the classes with their children. The manual contained numerous exercises and interactive experiences which the parents shared with their child. E.g. The children wash their parents' feet or the other way around.

The children learn topics which might be included in most baptismal blesses.

>   What is Baptism?

>   How can the Holy Spirit live in us?

Chapter 17. An Equipment Track for Children

Sons and Servants

Stewardship

Worship

The Vision of our church

Before they have finished they are asked to write their own testimony and explain why they wish to be baptised. Then they report back to the call group to share what has happened and to give their personal testimony.

At this time the cell group recommends that the child should be baptised in a Sunday service by one of the pastors and one of his/her parents. The cell group would be involved in the baptism and often they would have a small party afterwards.

Baptism is a highlight for a new Christian and a moment of deep commitment to God. It should not be rushed into before the child is ready, Neither should it be held back when the child's heart is turned towards God in obedience. Every child is different. The privilege of baptising your own child is a privilege not to be missed.

Stage 3:
2. Sermon Notes

In our church in Singapore many of the older Barnabas Club children kept a nice hardback notebook to write down their sermon notes when they were in church. In some services a Children's leader would write up a simple outline of the sermon on a screen. They would bring the notebook to the cell group and report what they had head from Pastor's message.

A sponsor or leader would check the notebooks for accuracy and understanding.

Stage 3:
3. Spiritual Warfare

It is not long before children discover that living as a Christian in our world is like living in a battle zone. Satan is only too willing to discourage our children and make them turn back from their commitment. They need to know how they can resist his temptations and attacks.

Spiritual Warfare classes were also led by Children's Ministry leaders in a church context. They had a manual which covers topics like these.

> What kind of battle is going on?
>
> Why does Satan want to discourage you?
>
> The armour of God
>
> Dealing with temptation
>
> Spiritual Gifts
>
> Using the power of the Holy Spirit
>
> Strategic Prayer.

The cell group would encourage the children to go to a Spiritual Warfare weekend. Sometimes it could be held in a camp. The amazing t hing is that every time we taught this course, the Holy Spirit made Himself very real to the children

Chapter 17. An Equipment Track for Children

and they had plenty of good news to report back to their cell group.

Stage 3:
4. Bible Overview

This stage was a private study module which the child could follow through in their own time. It did not give exhaustive coverage of the Bible but it helps the children fits the various parts of their teaching in place. Most church children know most of the popular Bible stories but they have no idea how they fit together. They do not know whether Moses comes before David or whether they lived at same time as Jesus. It all just happened, "in the olden days."

One young adult entering Bible college told me that he had only recently discovered that the Bible events took place over such a long time. He thought that whole thing happened in a special "holy age" which lasted about twenty years. Children are often like people who have all the pieces of the jigsaw puzzle shaken together in a large jar, but they have never been able to put the picture together.

Once the children understand what kind of book the Bible is and how they can find their way around it they will be liberated into using the Bible more effectively.

CONCLUSION

The vision of our Children's Ministry is to produce children who attain, *"full Christian maturity according to their age."* Our goal is that they should be *"worship leaders, prayer warriors, evangelists, sponsors, team leaders and ministry helpers."*

It is a systematic plan built around the idea of family leadership. The cell group has the role of encouragement and helping. For a while our children were issued with a Children's Equipping Log on which they record their own personal progress, The children did not have to be pressed into taking new steps. They wanted to know they were moving along towards growing up in Christ.

The way to judge the success of a children's Ministry is to look at the end product. Huge numbers on the roll do not prove success. When we see our children living happily in the presence of the Holy Spirit, and taking up leadership in the church and the cell group, we know we are fulfilling the vision which God has given us.

TO THINK ABOUT

1. Does your church have a systematic plan for helping your children to grow into maturity?

2. How can we help parents to carry out their spiritual leadership responsibilities towards their children?

3. What does your church hope to achieve in the lives of the children under your care?

www.ingramcontent.com/pod-product-compliance
Lightning Source LLC
LaVergne TN
LVHW020926090426
835512LV00020B/3229